A COMPARISON BETWEEN
WOMEN AND MEN

A COMPARISON BETWEEN WOMEN AND MEN

Tarabai Shinde and the critique of gender relations in colonial India

ROSALIND O'HANLON

OXFORD
UNIVERSITY PRESS

OXFORD

UNIVERSITY PRESS

YMCA Library Building, Jai Singh Road, New Delhi 110 001

Oxford University Press is a department of the University of Oxford. It furthers the
University's objective of excellence in research, scholarship, and education
by publishing worldwide in

Oxford   New York

Athens   Auckland   Bangkok   Bogota   Buenos Aires   Calcutta
Cape Town   Chennai   Dar es Salaam   Delhi   Florence   Hong Kong   Istanbul
Karachi   Kuala Lumpur   Madrid   Melbourne   Mexico City   Mumbai
Nairobi   Paris   Sao Paulo   Singapore   Taipei   Tokyo   Toronto   Warsaw

with associated companies in Berlin Ibadan

Oxford is a registered trade mark of Oxford University Press
in the UK and in certain other countries

Published in India
By Oxford University Press, New Delhi

ISBN 019 564 736X

Typeset by All India Press, Pondicherry 605 001
Printed by Saurabh Print-O-Pack, Noida
Published by Manzar Khan, Oxford University Press
YMCA Library Building, Jai Singh Road, New Delhi 110 001

Acknowledgements

I have benefitted from advice and help from many sources in the course of preparing this book. Warm thanks are due to Dorothy Stein, whose idea it was to translate Tarabai's text, and who provided valuable critical readings of the introductory essay. Kalini Deshpande and Ian Raeside were kind enough to go through my translation and to point out innumerable corrections and improvements, for which I owe them a special debt. My old friends Ram Bapat and Vidyut Bhagwat have been generous as always with their time and ideas. I also spent many diverting hours in discussion with David Washbrook, David Ludden and Chris Bayly, who made invaluable suggestions about the wider social historical context in which I have particularly wished to set this study. At various stages I have also benefitted greatly from discussions with Padma Anagol, Crispin Bates, Uma Chakravarty, Dipesh Chakrabarty, Partha Chatterjee, Alice Clark, Nick Dirks, Saurabh and Leela Dube, Geoffrey Elton, Pat Hilden, Manjiri Kamat, Julia Leslie, Tanya Luhrman, S. G. Malshe, Lata Mani, Liz Nissan, Y. D. Phadke, Gyan Prakash, Pratibha Ranade and Usha Thakkar.

I am grateful also to the Smuts Fund, the British Academy and the Nuffield Foundation for financial assistance in carrying out parts of this project, and to the staff of the Centre of South Asian Studies, Cambridge, the Oriental and India Office Collections, the British Library and the Mumbai Marathi Granthasangrahalaya for their efficient and material help. Lastly, my very warmest thanks are due to my colleagues at Clare for providing financial and moral support over many years.

Contents

Contents

Introduction

Some time towards the end of 1880, a local policeman in the small village of Olpad, near Surat in south Gujarat, heard rumours that a young widow of the village was pregnant. Her name was Vijaylakshmi, she was twenty-four years old and the daughter of a local brahman family. He paid her a visit, satisfied himself that the rumours were true, and reported the affair to the District Magistrate to prevent her from disposing of the child in secret. Nothing more was done, then, until March 1881, when the body of a new-born baby was found on a rubbish heap in the village. The local chief constable went immediately to see her and, convinced of her guilt, had her put on a bullock cart and taken to Surat. She confessed to the second class magistrate that she had given birth to the child, and to avoid shame had killed it by cutting its throat with a cooking implement. A Dubla servant woman had disposed of the body on to the rubbish heap. Vijaylakshmi was examined by the civil surgeon, then put back on the cart and returned later in the day to Olpad. In April of 1881, she was brought to trial before the local sessions judge, and sentenced to hang. The case was then heard before the Appeal Court in Bombay where, amidst sensational publicity, her sentence was mitigated to one of transportation.[1]

Vijaylakshmi's was not an uncommon case, particularly among brahman and other high caste Hindu women in nineteenth century India, married before puberty and encouraged to conform to a model of ascetic chastity if they were unlucky enough to lose their husbands. But Vijaylakshmi's case in particular, the attention she received and the way she was discussed in the press and in public debates, seem to have come almost as the last straw to one woman observer, prompting her to put pen to paper in a furious rebuttal. As Tarabai Shinde saw it, these public discussions of Vijaylakshmi and her horrible crime were symptomatic of much wider attitudes towards women in India, attitudes which she felt had become more pronounced during her own lifetime. She published the resulting book, *A Comparison between Women and Men*, in 1882.[2]

I came across this book when researching into other aspects of western India's social history, and it seemed interesting enough to be worth translating. As I soon discovered, however, this on its own did not seem to be enough. I therefore added the present essay as a means of 'translating' in a larger sense, to draw out themes from the text and explain what I understood to be their wider significance. What results is, I fear, a very awkward combination of translation and an introductory essay which is itself almost as long. Readers understandably averse to such a combination can find basic information about Tarabai in the first section of this essay, and thereafter read her text independently.

In trying to make sense of the text and of Tarabai's wider social milieu, I have been greatly benefitted by recent advances in the wider fields of women's history and gender studies in India, which have not only expanded rapidly themselves, but have added to our understanding of much broader processes of change in colonial Indian society. One important advance here has been our clear break with the old liberal interpretation of the debates over 'social reform' for women that were so widespread in India during the nineteenth century.[3] This interpretation, shaped by the modernization theory which dominated much post-war western historical writing about India, viewed such concern for women as little more than a natural response to the real disadvantages that Hindu 'tradition' in particular imposed upon them. Lata Mani and others have argued that 'women' actually appeared in this public discussion more as a symbol of the moral health of the 'tradition' itself, as this was debated among male colonial officials and missionaries, and Indian reformers, nationalists and conservatives, to the exclusion, very largely, of the views and voices of women themselves.[4]

Other historians have pushed forward our understanding of the influential new models for middle class female respectability that were emerging from the mid-century, amid a plethora of new periodical and pamphlet guides to the 'domestic' as women's peculiar sphere, with its own expertises of enlightened childcare, cookery, accounts and family education.[5] As Meredith Borthwick has pointed out, these models, clearest in the *bhadramahila* of late nineteenth century Bengali reformist circles, seem a peculiar amalgam of brahmanic and middle class Victorian social values, with their emphasis on wives that were at once selfless angels of the hearth and cultivated helpmeets to their husbands.[6]

This perspective links up with wider questions of social change. Some historians have suggested, convincingly, I think, that social and religious identities in colonial society may have become more caste-bound and 'brahmanic' in character than they were in pre-colonial India.[7] In this 'traditionalization' of colonial society, gender relations emerged as a powerful new means for the consolidation of social hierarchy and the expression of caste exclusivity. Gender may also have been a key element in the construction of colonial hegemony itself, shared idioms of femininity providing key groups of Indian and British men alike with a common language in which they were able to discuss and agree on important aspects of the Indian social order.[8] Others have identified areas of co-operation and agreement in the widespread assumption that politics and administration constituted a particular 'public' and masculine domain, as opposed to the domestic as a sacrosanct private realm of family and religion, a view that appealed not only to Victorian colonial officials, but to important classes of Indian men anxious to find means of preserving these areas of their own power against colonial intervention.[9] This in turn raises the much-debated issue of gender within Indian nationalist politics. In particular, as Partha Chatterjee and others have noted, questions of women's emancipation seemed to disappear from most nationalists' political agendas from the last decade of the nineteenth century, and it is by no means clear why.[10]

What makes all of these questions difficult to answer is in part the relative paucity for most of the nineteenth century of women's own testimony, particularly in matters of politics, power and their perceived relationships with men. For an important if obvious test of our answers to them lies in the extent to which they can encompass and explain women's own expressed views and experience. For these reasons we need more access to women's own writing in this period, and indeed there has recently begun to emerge a very good range of anthologies, translations and life histories for various parts of India, including historical as well as contemporary material.[11]

What, then, do we know about Tarabai Shinde, author of *A Comparison between Women and Men*? She came from a prosperous family of Marathas, one of western India's major agriculturalist communities. Like other social groupings that came to constitute 'dominant castes' in later colonial India, the Marathas had two centuries earlier been one of a number of pioneering peasantries who took advantage of the weakening of Mughal power to tighten their own hold on rural resources. At this period, the term 'Maratha' was itself actually very narrowly applied, to mark off those small numbers of elite families who aspired to the position of independent kings and the royal or *kshatriya* status that went with it. For the rest, most peasant cultivators identified themselves simply as *kunbi*, the local variant of one of India's generic and occupational terms for a farmer. As with other pre-colonial agriculturalist communities, the boundaries of the Maratha-*kunbi* complex were loose and permeable, enabling most people who took to settled agriculture to be assimilated over a period into *kunbi* networks of commensality and marriage. This social flexibility was a considerable advantage in the mobile and highly militarized society of late Mughal India. As the loosening of Mughal control from Delhi opened up regional state systems to new political competitors, power came increasingly to depend on their ability to attract and incorporate men and skills, and the success of warbands upon some principle at least of egalitarianism and brotherhood.[12]

As a loose agglomeration of armed lineages, small autochthonous gentry and mobile peasant cultivators doubling as military recruits during the campaigning season, the Marathas first emerged as a significant force in the fluid politics of the subcontinent in the mid-seventeenth century under the famous leadership of Shivaji Bhosle, son of a petty *jagirdar* of the Ahmadnagar Nizamshahi kingdom. Over the course of the eighteenth century, a number of key families (those, indeed, whom Tarabai mentions) had established themselves as important regional powers and 'little kings' in their own right, connected through ties of kin and clientship with a network of substantial local gentry. These prominent Maratha families, as well as their wider client communities of lesser gentry and humbler *kunbi* cultivators, were transformed during the early part of the nineteenth century into more village-based peasant communities, very much in line with the drive of the East India Company to make mobile and military people into sedentary and revenue-paying farmers. It was from this period that Marathas, in common with other 'warrior-peasant' communities in India, seem to have developed more rigid community boundaries against outsiders, and a stronger emphasis on status and hierarchy within it.[13]

We can date Tarabai's life with some precision, and have some basic information about it.[14] She wrote and published this, her only book, between 1881 and 1882, and a contemporary remembers her still living, as an elderly woman, about 1905. Her life, then, would have spanned most of the second half of the nineteenth century, and a little beyond. Her own family was one of four that formed the social elite of Buldhana, a small town of about three thousand people in the fertile alluvial cotton-growing tracts of Berar in central India. The family owned some land outside the town, but her father, Bapuji Hari Shinde, worked as a head clerk in the office of the Deputy Commissioner in the town. She was the only daughter in a family of five, and her father was reputed to have doted on her. He was also an early member of the Satyashodhak Samaj, the reformist and anti-brahman 'Truth-seeking society' set up in western India in 1873 by the Poona radical Jotirao Phule.[15] Phule was also a close friend of the family, and, as we shall see, an important and influential contact. Without her father's reformist commitments it is most unlikely that she would have learned to read or write: as it was, she did so not only in Marathi, but to some extent in English and Sanskrit also.

Despite these connections, it is also likely that the Shindes, as a respectable Maratha household, practised some form of seclusion for its women. Tarabai certainly refers to herself as someone who has been 'kept locked up and confined in the proper old Maratha manner'. The term she uses here, *marathmola*, refers in particular to the seclusion of Maratha women, although, as we shall see, this may well have been more of a nineteenth century innovation than an ancient or invariable principle.[16] Tarabai was married, but a *gharjavai* husband was found for her. This meant that her husband, whose name was also Shinde, came to live with her in her father's house, instead of the more usual Hindu joint family practice whereby brides left their natal homes and were absorbed into their husbands' households.[17] It is not clear why this arrangement was

made: with her four brothers, the immediate family was not short
of sons to manage its concerns. In her book, Tarabai herself refers
with some bitterness to wealthy fathers who arranged *gharjavai*
marriages for their daughters just so that they could keep them
with them at home, even though grooms procured in this way were
usually poorer and less well-educated. This might possibly have
been the reason for her own *gharjavai* marriage. But such a
marriage did at least mean that she would have enjoyed the
relatively larger freedoms of life with an indulgent father in her
own *maher* or natal home. If these were indeed her domestic
circumstances, they would have contributed very considerably to
Tarabai's being able to push her way into the masculine world of
reading, writing and publishing. For, as many contemporaries as
well as historians have noted, the most immediate opposition to a
woman's learning her letters in this period came usually from her
mother-in-law and senior women in the household.[18] Tarabai
outlived her husband, although it is not clear when she was left a
widow. The pair had no children, and she did not remarry. Nor, as
far as we know, did she ever publish again.

Two specific personal memories of her have been preserved.
The prominent Maratha politician, Barrister Ramrao Deshmukh,
was at school in Buldhana between 1901 and 1907. He remembered
how he and his boyhood friends lived on different sides of the
Shinde house, and how great was their terror each time they had to
run past it: in part, because of the pair of large dogs that guarded
the house, but much more lest the 'harsh grey figure' of Tarabai
herself should catch them. This was in 1905, when Deshmukh was
about twelve, and he also remembered going with his mother to
Tarabai's house, and the white sari that she wore indicating that
she was a widow.[19] Gadadhar Govind Pathak, a *vakil* of the town,
recalled having seen Tarabai at about the same time:

> She was a short and dumpy woman, with thick glass
> spectacles on her eyes. There was always a stick in her
> hand. She had her fields where the T.B. sanitorium now
> stands in Buldhana. She used to go off to her fields very
> spiritedly on foot; I never saw her ride a horse. Her face
> was very cruel-looking. She had a very fiery temper.
> Whenever she saw small children, she would chase after
> them, hitting at them with her stick. We children used to
> be very much afraid of her. We never saw her husband.[20]

These memories may well have been mediated and coloured by an adult male knowledge of Tarabai's outspoken venture into print. But they give us an insight into something at least of the reputation that she had acquired for herself towards the end of her life, as a hardy, independent and somewhat pugnacious woman, whose shortage of proper feminine qualities was probably due to too much reading.

Her text consists of 52 printed Marathi pages. It was printed in Poona, and sold for 9 annas, about average for a pamphlet of its size. It has no very clear internal structure: indeed, she says in her introduction that 'This is my very first effort, so the book has passages that are disconnected and fragmentary, and it's written in the rough and harsh language of Marathas of old'.[21] Yet her main points are clear. She has been stirred to fury, she explains, by the way in which it was always women who got blamed for every kind of evil and suffering in Indian society. With a strong sense of herself as a loner addressing a hostile male readership, she launches into a bitter denunciation of the men who were actually culpable. In reality, it was men who had destroyed Indian manufactures and sullied their own cultural traditions in their headlong rush to embrace those of their English rulers. It was male priests who had made up all sorts of absurd religious rules for women, such as the idea that widows should not be allowed to remarry, or the notion that *pativrata*, self-effacing devotion to her husband, should be the informing principle of a woman's life. It was male religious writers who tried to reinforce them, by making up all sorts of absurd stories about womanly virtue and sacrifice. And it was male reformers, politicians, journalists and writers who now demanded that women continue to conform to these rules, in a society where everything else was changing and the same men themselves were gaining a whole range of new rights and freedoms, habits of consumption and dress, and opportunities for work, education and travel. In short, it was men who monopolized all rights and freedoms for themselves, while women such as the widow Vijaylakshmi were loaded down with the blame for all of society's evils. To drive the point home, Tarabai quotes mockingly from older and nineteenth century texts that vilified women in just this way; and then goes through the list of their supposed moral failings to demonstrate that exactly the same points were much better made about men. At the same time and in strong contrast to the tone of her writing, it is clear that Tarabai continued to hold some rather conventional and old-fashioned ideas about women and their proper rights and duties. This ambivalence resonates throughout the text, and we see her sometimes struggling and sometimes playing ironically with the contradictory implications of what she has to say.

Here, then, we have a text of considerable interest. Of course, women's literacy and concerns of this kind in India were by no means new. As in other regions of India, the women beginning to write at this time had good precedents in a small but very long-standing tradition of female literacy and writing. Pre-colonial western India produced literate women of many different kinds: saint-poets of the region's important *bhakti* devotionalist tradition, regents and widows who ruled in their own right, the women of important political families, the daughters of pundits, accomplished courtesans.[22] Moreover, the *bhakti* saint-poets were extremely adept at using the tradition's anti-caste and anti-brahmanical arguments for their own purposes as women. Women such as Muktabai, sister of the great mediaeval saint Dnyandeva, Janabai the maidservant of his contemporary Eknath, Kanhopatra the sixteenth century dancing girl who found her god in Pandharpur, or Bahinabai the disciple of the seventeenth century saint Tukaram, all wrote of their sadness at their supposed spiritual unfitness within any brahmanic religious hierarchy, and turned to the loving personal god of *bhakti* for salvation and a sense of their own worth as women.[23]

While vernacular print culture developed throughout much of India from the early nineteenth century, it was not until the 1860s and 1870s that women began to write and publish in any numbers. Even then, a direct concern with questions of gender was uncommon. Tarabai's is the first text that I know of, for western India at least, in which a woman addresses herself so squarely and polemically at the question of women's relations with men. Some of her questions are historical and political, as she asserts that there has been a long-term loss in women's access to power, compounded by the emergence of a new and exclusively masculine sphere of public life. On another level, she deals with a range of very practical matters, with marriage mores and conventions concerning widowhood and purdah, women's education and personal mobility, domestic politics and problems in everyday marital and family relationships. She is also deeply concerned with the ways in which women were represented, in texts of classical literature, in newspapers and modern novels and plays, and with the processes through which these textual norms and models for women's behaviour came to be invented and imposed. Particularly interesting is her strong sense that women in nineteenth century society have been placed in a peculiarly invidious and impossible position, urged to conform to extraordinary models of wifely self-abnegation, mostly drawn from old books, in circumstances and with men that made it quite impossible for them to do so. When they failed in their task as bearers of unattainable ideals, their failure naturally expanded to encompass all of society's crimes and ills. And yet caught as they were in this cleft stick, women had no means of making themselves heard amongst the voices that constantly discussed them and constantly found them deficient. As I shall argue, Tarabai has here put her finger on a set of extremely important processes in colonial culture and gender relations.

My purpose here, then, is to explore these themes in her book, to illuminate and explain some at least of her concerns by setting out the background and circumstances in which they developed, and lastly to see how far this unusual commentary, with its insights into a woman's own experience, might extend or reshape our present understanding of gender relations in the nineteenth century. I shall also set her arguments in their Maratha context. This is important because of what many historians have observed to be the particularly liberal and relatively egalitarian nature of society for women in Maharashtra. Yet Tarabai herself assumed that she had something to say about more than just her own social circles. The purpose of her book, as she says in the introduction, is 'to defend the honour of all my sister countrywomen. I'm not looking at particular castes or families here. It's just a comparison between women and men'.[24]

GENDER AND 'SOCIAL REFORM' IN NINETEENTH CENTURY INDIA

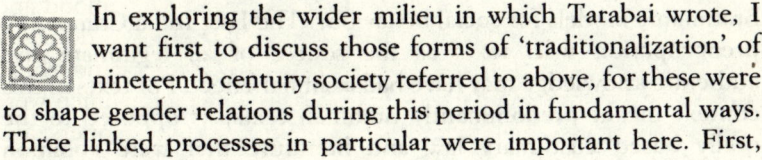
In exploring the wider milieu in which Tarabai wrote, I want first to discuss those forms of 'traditionalization' of nineteenth century society referred to above, for these were to shape gender relations during this period in fundamental ways. Three linked processes in particular were important here. First,

brahmanic religious values and religious texts appear to have become more widely diffused throughout Hindu society, extending what had been a narrowly applied model for social exclusiveness and respectability into one for much wider circles of upper and middle peasant castes, petty government employees, artisans and small tradespeople. Second, caste hierarchies seem to have grown more rigid and their boundaries less flexible and permeable. Third, and connected with this, questions of caste, 'custom' and family were from the very early Company period treated as private and changeless matters that were outside the normal purview of the state. Here, of course, East India Company strategies of rule were deeply affected by nineteenth century social theory and its division of social life into 'domestic' and 'public' spheres.[25]

At one level, of course, tendencies of this kind were not new. Many historians have seen these processes already in train in parts of late pre-colonial India, as emerging regional states sought to identify themselves more closely with their own local warrior-peasant communities, and brahman social groups, such as the Chitpavan brahman peshwa government of western India, came to pre-eminence as the demand intensified for their ritual and scribal skills.[26] Susan Bayly has explored the religious dimension of these processes, showing how until the later eighteenth century, the religious culture of the Tamil south had been a highly syncretic rather than a brahmanical one, incorporating a range of traditions: Saivite and Vaishnavite ritual, the worship of fierce female divinities associated with blood, battle and sacrifice, and popular veneration for local saints in which Hindus and Muslims alike shared.[27]

If some of these processes do seem to have been in train before the East India Company emerged as a major territorial power, others, as Christopher Bayly has described, had a more distinctly colonial origin.[28] The gradual replacement of Muslim by brahman service elites within the colonial administration throughout much of India helped to disseminate principles of hierarchy and more brahmanic models for social behaviour. The East India Company's preoccupation with texts as the source of all legitimate and authentic knowledge may have had a similar effect. For texts in this context meant predominantly brahman texts, as opposed to the orally based customary law and literature that were common outside literate circles.[29] Alongside these East India Company initiatives, moreover, were a whole range of Indian groups and movements. The Arya Samaj in north India, the Brahmo Samaj in Bengal or the Prarthana or Satyashodhak Samajes in the west also sought originality and authenticity in texts, as they attempted to 'purify' Indian social life and return it to its early noble simplicity.[30] Other factors may have affected the great warrior-peasant caste groups in particular. For them, the longer term and gradual replacement of labour in the eighteenth century by land in the nineteenth as a scarce resource, may have meant that the old political strategies of inclusion and incorporation gave way more decisively to an emphasis on exclusion and distinction. Amongst Rajputs, Jats, Patidars, Marathas and the like, community bound-aries seem to have become less permeable to outsiders, while different classes within them became more sharply concerned with demarcating gradations of status and wealth: between mere small peasant cultivators, new rich peasant farmers benefitting from the spread of cash crops, district-level office holders in the service of the raj, old aristocratic families who could trace their lineages back to the eighteenth century but were now increasingly impoverished, or had separated themselves off as an urban rentier or service class.[31]

Above all perhaps, these processes may have been intensified by the colonial government's own developing techniques of rule. The Pax Britannica in India effectively cut those links between caste identity and political power which had earlier kept such identities mobile and flexible. As many historians have noted, the East India Company learned rapidly to disguise its political function by declaring large areas of Indian society, including that of 'caste', to be private and changeless domains of tradition and custom, family and religion, where the state had no routine role and politics no place. This actually represented a very considerable contraction in the functions of state and ruler, which had both in Hindu and Indo-Muslim traditions of rulership intervened very actively in the regulation of a wide range of social and religious institutions.[32] This severance of domains formerly closely connected meant, of course, that new means had to be developed by which to incorporate key groups of Indians into the framework of colonial government. Increasingly from the mid-century, political representation, access to education and other forms of privilege came to depend precisely

on the assertion of clear and bounded caste identities, a task that
was most often undertaken by the 'caste associations' that prolif-
erated in India from about this time.[33] For all their rhetoric of
modernization and 'reform', these associations embodied just those
processes described above, typically combining an acute concern
to forge new forms of caste unity, identity and history, with an
effort to raise the status of the caste by disseminating new high-
caste forms of social practice.

Together, these processes were to have far-reaching implications for women. The intensification of social and caste competition
meant that marriage strategies and the control of women assumed
new importance as higher and middle peasant castes in particular
competed in the more crowded and static milieu of rural colonial
society. Particularly in Hindu cultural contexts where wife-takers
were more highly valued than wife-givers, these strategies and
forms of control could be crucial in establishing new patterns of
local caste dominance. Alice Clark, for example, has described
how marriage strategies and the limitation of women's numbers
helped in different ways to protect and consolidate the power of
Rajputs and Kanbis in Gujarat. For the former, it was of key
importance to limit the numbers of their women for whom
husbands had to be found, to avoid having to give them to social
inferiors. For the latter, keeping their numbers of marriageable
women static helped prevent the fragmentation of inheritance and
landholding in an increasingly densely populated agrarian economy.[34]
As caste groupings searched for new ways of expressing identity
and social distinction, moreover, the public conduct of their
women became paramount, and was judged according to standards
increasingly brahmanical in character.

Ideas of a realm of custom and family beyond the reach of the
state quickly entered the rhetoric of Indian politicians and reformers
themselves, with important effects for women. From the early years
of the century such ideas were used back against the colonial rulers
as a means of denying their competence in all such 'social' questions; later, nationalists developed it more positively to identify the
home and domestic life as the inviolate site of Hindu spiritual
values, as opposed to the gross materialism of colonial culture.[35]
These longer-term changes subordinated women more firmly to
caste and family authority, and consigned them to a domain of
'private life' supposedly outside politics. Thus seen as the very

embodiment of home and domestic life, 'woman' also became, as Lata Mani has described, the intensely discussed index of the tradition itself, her solid virtues a measure of its ancient strength, or, as liberals and reformers asserted, her ignorance and backwardness a sign of its deadly deficiencies.[36] This meant an intensifying public scrutiny of women's behaviour, just when women themselves were being excluded and pushed out of the 'public' domain.

Indeed, the social reform debates of the nineteenth century reveal an absolutely striking preoccupation with questions affecting women. With the exception, perhaps, of the issue of caste and untouchability, all major questions of the reform of Hindu society taken up at this period concerned women: *sati*, female infanticide, child marriage, the remarriage of widows, the seclusion and education of women, prostitution, brideprice and dowry. Let us now look at some of these campaigns and their consequences for women in western India in more detail.

Here as elsewhere in mid-century, the 'problem' of widow remarriage received an enormous amount of attention, discussed at length in the new vernacular press, in a spate of books and pamphlets and petitions to the Company government.[37] The 'problem' itself arose because brahmanic Hinduism placed enormous value upon womanly chastity and wifely devotion: a wife who was a true *pativrata* was an auspicious ornament to her family and an assurance of beatitude to her husband.[38] Brahman and other high castes in particular therefore viewed remarriage for women of whatever age as a source of embarrassment and social inferiority, and expected girls as well as older women to confine themselves to chaste and ascetic lives with their husband's families. Many women did so; others, like the widow Vijaylakshmi referred to above, disgraced themselves. Indeed, that widows were sexually available was both a social commonplace and a source of humour: the Marathi terms for widows and prostitutes were in many contexts interchangeable.[39] There were legislative as well as social obstacles in the way of women who wished to remarry: Hindu textual law, as expounded by the Anglo-Indian courts and embodied in a progressive accretion of case law, proscribed widow remarriage for higher castes and held the children of such marriages to be illegitimate. These marriages were finally recognized with the Hindu Widows' Remarriage Act of 1856, passed after an India-wide campaign led by the Bengali reformer, Ishwarchandra Vidyasagar.[40]

These issues were taken up most strongly in western India from the mid-century by the group of Bombay liberals who formed around the deist reform society, the Prarthana Samaj.[41] There were accompanying campaigns in the *Indu Prakash* newspaper, which had been set up in 1862 for the purpose by the leading politician and gradualist reformer M. G. Ranade, the prolific Marathi polemicist Gopal Hari Deshmukh and the uncompromising radical Vishnushastri Pandit. There was even a special society for the promotion of widow remarriage, set up in 1866. After the initial euphoria, however, all this produced rather little. The Act of 1856 certainly produced no rush of women remarrying; rather, the reformers had to search for volunteers or, as in the case of Vishnushastri Pandit, volunteer themselves. Amidst much invective and hostility, conservatives in the Bombay presidency formed a society of their own, the Hindudharma Vyavasthapak Sabha, and the two sides engaged in a series of public contests, culminating in Poona in 1870 with a formal debate presided over by the Shankaracharya of Karvir Math, one of western India's foremost arbiters of orthodox rectitude. Vishnushastri's party were declared in error, and, rather than risk social ostracism, most of them accepted the rituals of penance and purification prescribed by the Shankaracharya. Defeat followed on defeat. One of the few to resist recanting, M. G. Ranade, bowed to pressure from his family when his first wife died in 1873, and agreed not only to marry an eleven-year-old girl rather than a widow, but to bar his friend Vishnushastri from the house.[42]

With these setbacks, direct reformist efforts subsided for a decade, but, as elsewhere in India, questions of 'womanhood' still remained very much in the fore of public discussion. Most importantly here, there emerged in the 1870s, as in Bengal a decade earlier, a debate and consensus concerning the ways in which Indian and Hindu women might develop and transform themselves, whilst preserving what was best in 'traditional' culture. As Borthwick has described, the model of the *bhadramahila* emerged first amongst advanced reformist circles in Bengal and was then in diluted forms gradually disseminated elsewhere in urban middle-class India. This model for a new womanhood was a fusion of older brahmanical values of *pativrata*, of feminine self-sacrifice and devotion to the husband, with Victorian emphases upon women as enlightened mothers and companions to men in their own 'separate sphere' of the home. Such ideas had very considerable appeal. They were not really radical or threatening, either to older notions of female dependence or to the developing ideology of home and the domestic as sacrosanct domains of tradition and religion; in fact, they actually reinforced them. And for colonial India's emerging middle classes of government employees, professionals, teachers, journalists and the like, an 'educated' wife was rapidly gaining a range of attractions. She could be a career asset, in a social world that took women's education as a sign of civilized values. She could be an asset in running the new and more expensive types of household that many urban middle-class people were now establishing for themselves. Finally, employment in colonial administration in particular saw the gradual development of a much sharper distinction between work and home than existed in pre-colonial society. Home thus needed to be more of a haven from the peculiar cares of working in such an environment, with sympathy from a wife who understood something of its problems and disappointments.[43]

We can certainly see elements of these ideas emerging in western India during the 1870s in the circles around the Prarthana Samaj. M. G. Ranade, G. V. Kanitkar, who was a judge, reformer and translator of J. S. Mill's *The Subjection of Women*, the lawyer G. V. Joshi, and the novelist Hari Narayan Apte all tried to put them into practice by educating their own child-wives.[44] Together with their menfolk, and joined in 1882 from Bengal by the eminent young Sanskrit scholar Pandita Ramabai, these women founded the Arya Mahila Samaj, the 'Aryan Women's Society', as a basis for what was planned to be a much wider organization throughout the presidency. The new periodical press and other new print genres were also an important means for disseminating their ideas. In 1877, Moro Vitthal Walvekar, member of the Prarthana Samaj and editor of its *Subodha Patrika* newspaper, started Marathi's first periodical for women. This was *Grihini*, 'Housewife', and it was a typical example of the new vernacular journals for women now appearing in many parts of India.[45] Walvekar advertised it thus:

It has been deliberately started for women. Included in
the issues are subjects useful to women, such as the lives
of women from history and famous women from the

puranas, knowledge about nature, health and the
science of cooking, sewing work and the like. Some of
our learned friends have promised to write for us. Very
great care will be taken that the essays in the book
should always be mature, serious and restrained, and in
easy and straightforward language.[46]

Hari Narayan Apte's second novel, *Ganapatarava*, which was
serialized in *Manoranjana*, the monthly magazine that Kanitkar and
Apte started in July 1886, was also replete with these themes. The
start of the novel, for example, depicted an earnest discussion
between two Poona college students, one of whom was just reading
Mill's *Subjection*, about how marvellous it would be if husbands
and wives could be equal and mutually respected companions to
one another, each in their own spheres.[47]

The 1880s saw a return to more intensified controversy. The
beginning of the decade saw the emergence of the politicians Bal
Gangadhar Tilak and Gopal Ganesh Agarkar to public life, with
the foundation of their more outspokenly nationalist newspapers
Kesari and *Mahratta* in January 1881.[48] As nationalist opinion itself
became more self-conscious and better organized, questions
affecting women were debated with renewed intensity. The Parsi
reformer, Behramji Malabari, infuriated nationalists by publishing
lurid descriptions of the suffering caused by child-marriage, and
the hidden epidemic of sanguinary crime that was associated with
what he called 'enforced widowhood'. Pressing for legislative
intervention, he submitted two Notes to the government of India,
and the latter instituted in 1884 a broad process of public
consultation through presidency and local governments, to elicit
further information and opinion from 'such official or non-official
persons as were considered to be well-acquainted with native
feeling on the question'.[49] The weight of these masculine opinions
(no women were asked) was against state interference, and
Malabari's suggestions were dropped. Women's education, and in
particular the establishment of high schools for girls in Poona and
Bombay during the 1880s, also became a subject of acrimonious
controversy. Conservatives, Tilak included, urged that teaching
Hindu women to read would ruin their precious traditional virtues,
making them immoral and insubordinate. Liberals like Agarkar
countered with the view that in fact nothing could be done to

remedy the whole backwardness of Hindu society until women were educated, because women were at once the foremost victims and the strongest defenders of the status quo.[50] Antagonisms grew still more bitter over the case of Rakhamabai, the educated daughter of a Bombay doctor who in 1887 refused to go and live with the much older husband to whom she had been married as a child. Sued by her husband who demanded the return of his promised wife as his lawful property, Rakhamabai was first tried and acquitted under the ordinary civil law and given her freedom. This sparked a wave of conservative fury, and on appeal the Chief Justice ruled that she should be tried under Hindu law, which she was, and ordered to return to her husband.[51]

These tensions converged with particular intensity around the figure of Pandita Ramabai herself. For conservatives, of course, she was a startling and uncomfortable figure: a widow of twenty-four, an excellent Sanskrit scholar, a woman with pronounced views on the position of women in Hindu society, and finally, in 1883, a highly publicized convert to Christianity, on the grounds that it made no distinction of spiritual worth between men and women in the way that Hinduism did.[52] However, it was not merely the fact of her conversion that sparked off so much public hostility. Nor was it her heretical suggestion that Rakhamabai's case revealed a positive alliance between the colonial government and Indian men in questions involving women, or that the most strident nationalist demands for free speech and political rights tended to be made by men firmly opposed to such things for their own womenfolk.[53] Rather, as Ram Bapat has argued, her very public condemnations of the consequences of 'respectable' domestic life for Hindu women caused fury most of all because they hit precisely against nationalist attempts to identify the home as a sacrosanct domain for Hinduism's innermost 'spiritual' values.[54]

It was also clear that these pressures and disagreements would impinge directly on nationalist political organizing itself. It was therefore, of course, that the early founders of the Indian National Congress made it very clear that it was to be a purely political organization, eschewing 'social' questions and problems as matters purely for internal resolution within the different communities themselves. These lines were drawn even more firmly in 1887, when Ranade and others helped establish the National Social Conference as a separate platform for the discussion of social issues, to be held after the main annual meeting of the Congress, which would enable it to attract delegates as well as to make use of the same pavilion. Even this slender connection, however, proved too much, and particularly in the context of the more aggressively Hindu and revivalist themes that spread through nationalist politics through the 1890s. Fearful of alienating the Congress's wealthy conservative supporters at its Poona session in 1895, and fiercely opposed to the reformers' having 'nationalist' pretensions or associations of any kind, Tilak campaigned successfully to have the National Social Conference barred from using the Congress pavilion.⁵⁵ In this climate, 'social reform' issues for women receded from the forefront of nationalist and political debate.

Having sketched in this background and some of its wider implications for women, let us turn now to look at Tarabai Shinde's own more immediate social milieu. This was in some ways rather different from the predominantly brahman reformist and nationalist circles described above, and, as we shall see, Tarabai viewed both of these with scepticism and hostility. This was certainly in keeping with the politics of the Satyashodhak Samaj in which her family was immersed, and which had itself been established amongst prosperous merchant and lower Maratha service people to contest the growth of brahman power within British administration, and of brahman social values within Indian society more generally. While these were the basic concerns of the Samaj and its founder Jotirao Phule, questions concerning women were important for them in several ways. Like all other reformers, they emphasized the importance of women's education for the wider uplift of 'backward' caste communities like their own. Denouncing 'brahmanic' practices such as child-marriage and the prohibition of widow remarriage could also be a powerful means of attacking brahmans. At the same time, as we shall see, Marathas were as much concerned as other caste communities about dignifying their social practice and to mark themselves off more clearly from social rivals in rural and urban contexts alike through the behaviour of their women.

Certainly Phule himself had a considerable interest in a range of issues concerning women, whom he presented as victims of brahmanic culture and power in common with other lower caste and untouchable people. From 1848, he and his wife Savitribai ran a school for girls in Poona, for which his father threw them out of the house.[56] During the 1860s, he ran a 'home' in his own compound for pregnant brahman widows, which was advertised provocatively by means of notices pasted up publicly in the brahman quarter. He was very clearly adept at using women's issues in this provocative way: one of his friends recalled, for example, how he deliberately employed an old brahman woman, Gangubai, on very large wages, as a servant in his house, as a way of mocking the wealthy brahmans who usually employed poor women from other castes to do their menial work. He seemed to have succeeded, for Gangubai's relatives came to Poona and took her away.[57] In the early 1880s he was drawn into the controversy over Pandita Ramabai. His pamphlet *Satsar*, 'Essence of Truth', published in September 1885, defended her against critics of her conversion, and referred also to Tarabai as another valiant defender of women's rights and dignity. He described how:

> Today, through the power of the English rulers, a few of the harassed womenfolk of this country have begun hesitatingly to learn to read and write. So in this issue a small effort is made to lay out before women's eyes all of the evil men's tricks through which the cunning Aryans have for thousands of years tormented all women in all sorts of ways, and still do so now.[58]

He defended Ramabai, pointing out that brahmans had always invented all sorts of mischievous lies about women and stopped them from being educated for fear that this would make daughters-in-law too rebellious. But he also pointed out that she had not been the first, because 'before Pandita Ramabai came to Poona, Mrs Tarabai Shinde of Buldhana in Berar, wrote a book called "A Comparison between Women and Men"'. Referring intimately to Tarabai as *chiranjivi*, 'our dear daughter', he explained that she had intended the book to express the anger that many women felt at their ill-treatment by menfolk, and to spell out to men what they needed to do to recover their women's affection and loyalty.[59]

It is clear, then, that Tarabai and Phule shared much in common, both in their hostility to orthodox religion, and in the language they used to condemn it. Indeed, Satyashodhak language seems to have provided her with a kind of dictionary which she deployed for her own purposes, its highly-coloured images of cunning and lustful brahmans reappearing in her own rhetoric as cunning and lustful men as such. For Phule, brahmanic religion oppressed lower caste people because it had been devised by brahmans; for Tarabai, it oppressed women because it had been devised by men. Yet other aspects of her life and writing mark it off very sharply from Satyashodhak political culture, in ways which clearly reflect her greater political marginality as a woman: her sheer irreverence and mockery of all, and not just brahman male authority, her disdain for idealized models of feminine respectability, and her sense of isolation as a writer and defender of women's dignity before a readership and political audience that she assumed to be almost exclusively masculine. Issues such as education, remarriage or the seclusion of women mattered to her also because they had an immediate and practical bearing on real women's circumstances, rather than as disguised political ammunition for other causes. What seems extraordinary, indeed, and to underline the very different implications for women even of a radical political movement like the Satyashodhak Samaj, is that the Shinde household still practised some sort of seclusion for its women, as Tarabai complains at the start of her book.[60] Here, as on the issue of women's rights to remarriage, her point was not just that things were difficult for women in comparison with the increased freedoms that men enjoyed in colonial society, but that they were actually getting worse. I want to turn now to explore these parts of her argument, and to suggest that they might best be understood in the wider context of processes of 'traditionalization' referred to above.

TRADITIONALIZING WOMEN: SECLUSION
AND REMARRIAGE IN THE NINETEENTH CENTURY

Like 'caste', the practice of purdah has often been regarded as very much a feature of 'traditional' India.[61] Yet there is much evidence that for 'warrior-peasant' people like the Marathas, purdah came actually to be more rigidly enforced during the nineteenth century, as well as acquiring a more distinctively Hindu rather than Muslim form. As H. Papanek and others have argued, it is possible very broadly to distinguish different rationales underlying the two, although in practice they often merge. For

Muslims, the veiling of women with the *burqa* before outsiders emphasizes the unity of a trusted circle of kin; for Hindus, veiling is practised within the home as well as outside, and relates rather to relations of authority and respect amongst affines, particularly between a woman's natal family and that of her husband, within which she was required to show considerable modesty and deference, especially in her early married life. This suggests, as Papanek points out, that for Hindus purdah was not simply an alien measure adopted at the time of the Muslim invasions; for Hindus it was and is an elaborate means of signalling female modesty and obedience.[62]

What is much less clear, however, is the extent to which the seclusion of 'respectable' women was actually consistently practised in the mobile and highly militarized societies of late pre-colonial India. It has become a historical commonplace that the Marathas secluded their women as a result of their long association with Mughal court culture. An early Marathi dictionary of 1829 thus defined *marathmola*, 'the true old Maratha custom' as meaning 'the practice whereby the women of those who call themselves Marathas have to wear the burqa'.[63] Yet, for western India at least, it is striking how far eighteenth-century commentators agreed that women were seldom veiled. A late-eighteenth-century Persian manuscript recorded that 'the women of all ranks, both rich and poor, go unveiled; and those of distinction go in palankens without curtains. The wives of soldiers ride about on horseback'.[64] Colonel Tone, who commanded a regiment of the Maratha peshwa's army, wrote in 1798 that he had seen the daughters of princes in the field sitting making bread with their own hands and 'otherwise employed in the ordinary business of domestic housewifery'.[65] The writer of a history of the Maratha Bhosle family in 1801 recorded that 'the Mahratta women expose themselves more than the women of other parts of India, and the greatest of them are frequently on horseback; nay, some are said to lead armies and mix in battle'.[66] Perhaps the closest observer of women in the Maratha camps was Thomas Broughton, who spent a year with the army of Mahadaji Shinde in 1809. He reported that

> A Mahratta line of march exhibits a collection of the
> most grotesque objects and groups that can possibly be
> imagined; and at no time is the difference in the
> treatment of women, between the Mahrattas and other

natives of India, more strikingly displayed. Such as can afford it here, ride on horseback, without taking any pains to conceal their faces; they gallop about and make their way through the throng with as much boldness and perseverance as the men. Among the better sort it is common to see the master of a family riding by the side of his wife and children, all well-mounted, and attended by half a dozen horsemen and two or three female servants, also on horseback; and I have often seen a woman seated astraddle, behind her husband, and keeping her seat with no small degree of grace and dexterity.[67]

'The Mahratta women', he said, 'are generally speaking, very ugly; and have a bold look which is to be observed in no other women of Hindoostan'. Interestingly, however, Broughton's remarks do suggest some form of public veiling in the Shinde camp. The women wore 'when abroad a Chadur or large veil, and sometimes a shawl, which envelops the whole figure'.[68] This may reflect Shinde's particularly close ties with the north Indian Muslims and Rajputs who came to dominate his armies during the years of his campaigning in northern India. Richard Jenkins, resident at the Maratha court of Nagpur in the 1820s, reported, on the other hand, that 'The Maratha women are under little personal restraint. They appear unveiled in public'.[69]

It may well have been, then, that, for all the aura of tradition surrounding the term *marathmola*, its eighteenth century existence was partial and interrupted. What should have changed to make the seclusion of women more widespread in the course of the nineteenth century? For all those who moved to the expanding new towns, it may have seemed an important means of protecting a family's dignity in a strange environment where familiar social markers were lacking. This was certainly the case in other parts of India, where there are also hints that a more 'Hinduized' form of seclusion was taking hold. The Bengal government servant Mirza Abu Taleb Khan wrote in 1801 that

> Before the Mussulmans entered Hindustan, the women did not conceal themselves from view; and even yet, in all the Hindu villages, it is not customary; and it is well known how inviolable the Hindus preserve their own

custom, and how obstinately they are attached to it; but now so rigidly do the women in the great towns observe this practice of concealment from view, that the bride does not even show herself to her father-in-law, and the sister comes but seldom into the presence of her brother.[70]

Other factors may have worked in the same direction. The more sedentary and demilitarized society that the East India Company strove to create clearly removed those aspects of geographical mobility that may have prevented military families from imposing seclusion in a rigid way. Perhaps most powerfully, those processes described above making for more rigid and bounded caste communities in a more static colonial social order may have impelled the great agricultural castes in particular to adopt this potent new means of expressing their social standing.

Certainly from mid-century at any rate, contemporaries refer increasingly to *marathmola* as a practical reality, a reality that, significantly, appeared now to be taking a more Hinduized form. Writing in 1861, the social critic Tukaram Tatya Padval observed that

> The Marathas lived within the Muslim state, and so they adopted many of their practices. What is called 'marathmola' really only means keeping women in purdah. If a woman cannot ever meet her father or brother when they come to visit, who can she see! Even if the Marathas fall on very hard times, they will not allow the women out of doors, and because there are no servants in the house, the men have to do it themselves.[71]

This kind of feminine modesty was, of course, still difficult to impose and not always successful. A disapproving correspondent to the *Dnyanodaya* newspaper wrote in the same year that

> Some Marathas and other vulgar people among us, when their sister-in-law comes to visit, stand right out in the road, and exchange such conversation and gestures with their hands that I feel ashamed to write about it. What happens to their marathmola then?[72]

It was a commonplace in almost all the Bombay presidency Gazetteers of the early 1880s that all those gentry, village headmen and large landholders now claiming descent from the ancient royal Maratha houses, adopted *marathmola* and secluded their women. In Sholapur district it was reported that

> When going out women of the higher Maratha families cover themselves from head to foot in a broad white sheet which prevents any part of the face from being seen. This is commonly known as the Maratha mola, or Maratha practice. They do not work out of doors, the water being brought home by servants or the men of the house. An upper class Maratha woman on no account shows her face before strangers.

These families also refused to remarry their women, unlike ordinary *kunbi* agriculturalists, whose women helped their husbands in the fields and could remarry after the death of a spouse.[73] In Satara, 'the well-to-do strictly enforce the women seclusion system called ghosha, that is curtain, or Marath mola, that is, Maratha custom'.[74] In Nasik, 'rich Marathas do not allow widow remarriage, strictly enforce the zenana system, goshe, and wear the sacred thread which is given them at marriage'.[75] The Ahmadnagar Gazetteer described the domestic arrangements of these Maratha gentry:

> Marathas live in better class houses with brick walls and tiled roofs. Those whose women do not appear in public divide the house into two; the back part called the janankhana is given entirely to the use of women and the front called the devadi or vestibule is used by the men.[76]

Purdah in these contexts was clearly part of a more Hinduized system for the expression of female modesty within the house as well as without. This was reflected in the interior dress of Ahmadnagar Maratha women, who used the *padar*, the end of the sari, not only to cover the shoulders and head, but also to veil the face.[77] In Tarabai's own district of Berar, it was reported that Marathas

> observe the parda system with regard to their women, and will go to the well and draw water themselves rather than permit their wives to do so; but the poorer Marathas cannot maintain the system and they and their wives and children work in the fields.[78]

The strength of purdah amongst Marathas naturally attracted considerable criticism, not least from their brahman political rivals who made much of the absurdity of these Maratha attempts at social dignity. Articles in the *Kesari* newspaper in 1882, for example, suggested that purdah had never originally been a rule amongst the Marathas, but that somehow, perhaps from their association with the Muslim ruling power,

> the belief must have spread that women who go out of doors are poor, ill-born and coarse; and so out of pride some began to make a fuss about their women not going out. Even if they are not able to bring food to eat, the water needs fetching, or the women need their saris washing, they think it's all very good!

Now, the writer went on, 'Amongst royal Maratha houses such as that of Shinde, Holkar and Gaikwad, and amongst some other Marathas who call themselves high-born, the authority of this custom is enormously strong'. Marathas defended seclusion in different ways. Some said that 'their morals and pativrata are the greatest ornament of women, and in order to protect them, this custom can never be abandoned': a ridiculous argument, because it implied that women who were not veiled were all immoral. Other promoters of veiling for women were simply extreme misogynists, 'thoughtless philosophers who hate women and say that women's carnal desires exceed those of men eight times over, and if they are not thus put in awe, the very next day they will run away hand in hand with someone else'. The writer concluded that 'some Marathas of education and understanding must have felt complete contempt for this barbaric practice, but out of fear of public hostility have each died in his place without doing anything about it'.[79]

In central India and Tarabai's own district, we can follow this interplay very closely between caste, the local rivalries of old and new rural elites, and the development of new models for respectable women's behaviour. A number of commentators emphasized the declining fortunes of the old Maratha military aristocracy of the region, families who had accumulated land and property in the service of pre-colonial states and now found themselves trying to maintain some semblance of their old styles of living on ever more divided shares of their old estates.[80] Alongside these were evidently a rising group of newer Maratha gentry, who were employed as magistrates, members of district and taluka boards, who held large estates, and had in many cases titles of *deshmukh* granted them by the British in recognition of their services.[81] These families now tried to constitute themselves into a separate and superior caste of Maratha Deshmukhs, with the behaviour of their women a key mark of their status. In Buldhana district in 1910, it was recorded that Deshmukhs had developed

> into a sort of aristocratic branch of the caste and marry among themselves when matches can be arranged. They do not allow the marriage of widows nor permit their women to accompany the wedding procession. A Deshmukh Sabha has been formed for Berar, one of its aims being to check intermarriage with ordinary kunbis.[82]

Older Maratha families of the region, led by Nilkanthrao Bhausaheb Khalatkar, himself a Deshmukh and honorary magistrate and district council member from Nagpur, strongly resisted the efforts of these low-born office-holders to try to convert their titles into a superior caste status. Khalatkar pointed out that 'a deshmukh is a title given by the government, it is not to be thought of as a caste. And it is also not to be thought that real Marathas have a lower rank because they are not Deshmukhs'. It was also not true that the marriage and other social practices of Marathas and ordinary *kunbi* families were the same: for the latter allowed second marriages, did not keep purdah, and did not put on the sacred thread, all things which Marathas did. The fact was that 'kunbi deshmukhs are really just kunbis, though kunbi deshmukhs themselves do not agree'.[83] As for Marathas themselves, he lamented the spread of seclusion amongst rich and poor alike:

> Today among the Marathas, there is such terrible purdah, that women do not even give water to the men of their own house, young or old. So how can they appear at their married homes before fathers-in-law or brothers-in-law? This is absolutely against nature. To put on purdah before the men of the house is nothing but a sort of prison. It means that the men have to work like slaves in front of the women who are in purdah, and women themselves become lazy. If there is just one man and one woman in the house and a friend or

relation comes, and there is either no one else at home
or the house is a poor one, then the man himself has to
go to the well like a woman, draw water and bring it
back on his head, while she is in the house doing
housework or cooking, and the friend or relation has
then to be sat down to eat on his own, and he has to
serve him, so that all in all, having purdah is more a
cause of sorrow than of happiness.[84]

Even poverty was no deterrent, for 'women of poor families go out
to the fields, and then when they come home, they put on purdah.
What is the point of that sort of purdah?'[85]

Interestingly, Khalatkar's recommendation for alternative
models for female behaviour begins to reflect the updated and
'Victorianized' ideal wife that we have already encountered in
liberal circles, where external social constraints were replaced by
internal ones of proper feminine modesty and self-control. Thus,
he urged,

Purdah should not be taken to extremes. Women
should not appear before people outside, but they
should be able to appear before household people using
a burqa or padar in a moderate way. They should not
giggle, and they should not talk too much. They should
not make jokes. They should not behave rudely to
anyone. Purdah should never be completely abolished,
but women should be able to go before their relatives
and own family using their padar. They should not just
speak to any old Tom, Dick or Harry. They should not
go completely bare-headed, or with their faces in full
view, whether they are at home or not.[86]

The danger, he urged, was that if there was not a reformed purdah
of this kind, then 'it is purdah in front of the father, and behind it,
+ + +'. The best thing of all would be 'if women were given
education in order to behave themselves in proper bounds and to
act with good morals'.[87]

Purdah in western India, therefore, may well have been very
much a nineteenth century creation, as western India's rural
Maratha gentry and their rivals amongst the newly wealthy competed to mark out their status and sharpen up their marriage
strategies in an increasingly crowded and static rural environment.

Moreover, these more Hinduized forms of purdah were relatively cost-free, for they did not even require womenfolk to withdraw from labour on the family farm. Poorer families whose women had to work could make the point just as easily by the strict seclusion of their women before elders, menfolk and visitors within the home. More research is needed, but there is some evidence at least to suggest that India's other large agricultural caste groups were moving in a similar direction. Sherring reported that it was only from the early nineteenth century that the Jats, for example, stopped intermarrying with members of lower agricultural castes, and began to seclude their once-free women.[88] David Pocock has described how Kanbi women in Gujarat were increasingly secluded and confined from the early nineteenth century, as patidar factions grew more competitive and greater stress was placed on the purity of women.[89]

If indeed new forms of female seclusion were developing in these ways, they might explain something of the anger and perturbation that observers like Tarabai would have felt as they surveyed the emerging contrast between men's and women's freedoms in colonial society. As she remonstrated with her male readership,

> You shut women up endlessly in the prison of the home, while you go about building up your own importance, becoming Mr, Sir and so on... Right from your own childhood you collect all rights in your own hands and womankind you just push in a dark corner, shut up in purdah, frightened, sat on, dominated as if she was a female slave. And all the while you go about dazzling us all with the light of your own virtue. Learning isn't for women, nor can they come and go as they please. Even if a woman is allowed to go outside, the women she meets are all ignorant like her, they're all just the same. So how's she to get any greater under-standing or intelligence?[90]

If purdah was one major concern for Tarabai in these emerging new Hindu models of female respectability, rights to remarriage and the social status of widows were others. Some historians have made the point that the institution of *sati*, widow burning, has only affected a tiny minority of Indian women, quite out of proportion to the attention colonial rulers and historians alike have paid to it.[91] Much the same point might be made about widowhood. What may also be important, however, is the way in which both *sati* and restrictions on remarriage helped to disseminate and reinforce models for female self-abnegation and deference to a much wider audience of Indian women than were ever directly affected by either. Tarabai herself certainly makes the point that it is not merely the social difficulties of widows themselves that concerned her, but the way in which the dread of widowhood shaped the behaviour of all married women.[92]

In many social contexts, of course, where women gain their identities principally as wives and mothers, widows and particularly younger or childless widows have constituted a special 'problem'.[93] This was particularly so in brahmanic religious culture, where, as we have seen in the case of Rajputs and patidars, 'surplus' women such as widows who had to be remarried could constitute a serious threat to a community's social and material standing. In this context, as Julia Leslie has described, older brahmanic ideals laid great emphasis on a wife's obedience to her husband during his life and her continued faithfulness to him beyond his death. The ideal wife, the *pativrata*, is one whose duties, purposes and identity derive entirely from her husband.[94] As enjoined in Sanskrit texts such as the Institutes of Manu and their vernacular reworkings, her husband is a wife's spiritual guide and her personal god. This relation of worshipper and god is expressed in rules for dress and ornament. A man's sacred thread and the signs on his forehead mark out his own religious affiliation, while the symbols of a woman's married state—the *kumkum* on her forehead, her bangles and the *mangalsutra* fastened round her neck during the marriage ceremony, indicate that her personal god is alive and there to ensure her social and ritual status as worshipper.[95] This relationship also emerges in contrasting notions of *dharma* itself. Whereas the masculine form *svadharma*, 'one's own *dharma*', refers generally to right action and religious duty in a broad sense, *stridharma*, the *dharma* or religious duty of woman, means *pativrata*, a chaste wife's devotion to her husband.[96] These connected ideas in turn meant that untimely widowhood represented an extreme of ill-luck and impurity. As the eighteenth-century Maratha pandit Tryambaka put it, 'Just as the body, bereft of life, in that moment becomes impure, so the woman, bereft of her husband, is always impure, even if she has bathed properly. Of all inauspicious things, the widow is the most inauspicious'.[97] Even the contemplation of remarriage would violate her *pativrata*; the only hope for a widow lay in ascetic self-denial until she could be reunited with her husband after death.

It is much more difficult to ascertain how far these attitudes to remarriage actually shaped social practice. They were widespread amongst brahmans in western India in the eighteenth century although, as Kadam has noted, the public campaigns against the remarriage of brahman widows suggests that widow celibacy may have been more of an ideal than a reality for some families at least. It was also a key point of contention between the peshwa's Chitpavan brahman community and their political rivals in the Sonar and Prabhu castes, who sought to enhance their status by preventing their women from remarrying, and were ordered by the peshwa to give their women freedom in this respect.[98] One way in which elite Maratha families in the eighteenth century marked their political arrival was also by restricting remarriage. Beyond these very narrow elite groups, however, women appear to have been able to remarry without difficulty.[99]

What is less clear, however, is how far this continued to be true through the nineteenth century. Early colonial observers certainly saw that remarriage carried something of a social stigma. In his description of the Deccan village of Lony in 1823, Thomas Coats reported that widows were sometimes permitted to remarry, 'but it is looked on by some families as disreputable, and not practised. It is only widowers who marry widows, and the offspring is not entitled to inherit in the same proportion as those by a first marriage'.[100] The reformer Balshastri Jambhekar reported in similar terms a decade later, that

> with the exception of a few very superior castes, second
> marriages may take place; though many of those who
> have no religious obstacle to enjoy that liberty, consider
> it a degradation to exercise it, in their love of imitating
> the higher classes.[101]

For the British themselves during the 1820s, this early picture was confused because they were still trying to distinguish between 'high' castes whose affairs should be regulated by the book law of the *shastra*s, and lesser communities whose practices were

enshrined in customary law. Assembling his legal digest for the
Bombay Deccan in 1826, Arthur Steele noted that 'the custom of a
second and inferior marriage, allowed to wives and widows in
many castes' was one of the main differences between the two:
'The second marriage of a wife or widow (called Pat by the
Mahrattas and Natra in Goozerat) is forbidden in the present age
at least, and to twice-born castes. But it is not forbidden to
Soodrus'. The prohibition of widow remarriage, Steele reported,
also distinguished well-born Maratha families from ordinary
agriculturalists: 'Such of them as are high Mahratta (as are the
families of the Sattara Raja, and other houses of pure Mahratta
descent) do not allow their widows to form Pat'.[102] With the
emergence of more organized social reform movements from the
1860s, it became something of a commonplace that this was
primarily a brahman problem: reflected, for example, in Pandita
Ramabai's concern with the 'high-caste' Hindu widow. Historians
have often tended to assume the same.[103]

What is striking in Tarabai's text, however, is her insistence
that the practice was actually spreading to a much broader range of
middling communities:

> It's just not true these days that only the brahman castes
> stop their widows getting married again. Lots of other
> castes and families do the same: Prabhus, Shenvis,
> Gujaratis, Bhatias, Marwadis, Marathas, Desais, Desh-
> mukhs, Inamdars; and Marathas with names like Shirke,
> Mahadik, Jadhav, Bhosle and Mane, families from
> places like Sholapur, Satara, Pune, Gwalior and Indore,
> the very families who died for the Maratha power. You
> can see an even stricter rule than the brahmans in their
> families against the remarriage of widows. In these
> people's houses you can wait till the end of your life and
> it won't happen. If one husband goes off and dies, too
> bad—they'll never let you have another one.[104]

Rates of remarriage for the nineteenth century are, of course,
extremely difficult to estimate, since it was not until the Census of
1881 that provincial governments began routinely to enumerate
marriage and widowhood. Yet there does seem to be some
evidence to suggest that from mid-century a much wider range of
people were beginning to incorporate restrictions on remarriage

into their social practice. Admittedly much of this evidence is fragmentary and anecdotal, but it comes from a remarkably wide range of sources. The silk-weaving Khatris of Bombay, for example, did not remarry their women, as a correspondent to their caste newspaper, the *Vichardarpan*, lamented in 1860.[105] Tukaram Tatya Padval reported of the Bombay Sonar goldsmiths that 'until quite recently, these people were accustomed to *pat* marriages of their widowed women, but within the last twenty years, the custom has been absolutely stopped'.[106] The Panchkalshes, an inferior writer people of Bombay, looked as though they were going in the same direction: 'These people still have the custom of marrying widows with *pat*, but within the last ten years, Hari Keshavji and other respected and influential gentlemen in the caste have been carrying on efforts to get the practice stopped'.[107] The Bhandari toddy-tappers of Bombay shared the same reluctance, for 'even though they still have the practice of *pat*, they feel ashamed when they remarry their widowed girls'.[108] As another Bhandari explained, his caste fellows often got these attitudes when they went off to work for the government and mixed with high caste employees: 'Some people just get a bit of education, then go off to do government and other service, and it's amongst these people that all these pure practices have spread, by their mixing together with superior castes'.[109] In 1865 the *Dnyanodaya* reported the suicide of a young brahman widow, adding that while it was certainly true that brahmans did not allow remarriage,

> the bar has not just stayed limited to them alone; within the last few years, even Sonars, Prabhus, Khatris, Panchkalshes and other such castes who behave like the brahmans have basically out of pride got their feet well and truly stuck fast in the vices of this custom.[110]

Many of the male respondents to the government of India's enquiries in 1884 argued that recent years had seen changes in the practice of lower castes. Shantaram Narayan, a pleader in the High Court of Bombay, reported that

> Widow remarriage being disallowed among the latter as sinful, the lower classes, though exempted from the ban, intuitively, as it were, learn to look upon it with some prejudice: and, in illustration of this, one could mention non-brahman communities among whom widow

remarriage was allowed, and prevailed formerly but who have, within living memory, declared themselves against the custom.[111]

Venkut Rango Katti, a translator in the Education Department from Dharwar, reported having seen similar instances:

> Shaved widows wearing red cloth can be seen in numbers among the Komties, the Kasars, the Sonars and the Gingars. I have read a long letter in the last month written by a Lingayat priest of Hoobli to one of the Canarese priests of Dharwar, in which the writer condemned widows remarried, freely availed of by his sect, as a stepping stone to hell, and invited his castemen to adopt widow celibacy which he praised in the most alluring way.[112]

Ramchorlal Chotalall reported that 'there are many castes of the Hindu community, such as the Kunbees, in which widow remarriage is freely allowed; but even among that caste there are some families who would not remarry their widows on account of the respectability of the family'.[113] The surgeon Sakharam Arjun reported that '"Enforced widowhood", though an institution of a pretty long standing among the brahmanical classes, has been of comparatively recent origin in the other castes', and had arisen, he said, 'due to that rage for imitating their superiors which constantly seizes an inferior class'.[114] With much disapproval, Satyashodhak activists noted the same trend. Narayanrao Lokhande reproached some of his Mali and Maratha caste fellows 'among whom there was the custom of widow remarriage, and now, imitating what the brahmans say, they have given up remarrying young widows'.[115] Jotirao Phule observed that 'because the Aryan brahmans brought this custom into use, impressionable and ignorant farming people, sonars and other castes have taken up their example, and so their daughters-in-law fall into difficulties in just the same way as the brahmans'.[116]

All of this is very difficult to back with any hard evidence, and I do not want to press the argument too far. However, the first large-scale figures for female widowhood that we have, those of the 1881 Census, do seem to point in the same direction. The following table gives figures for male and female widowhood in the Deccan region of the Bombay presidency for a cross-section of caste groups.

MALE AND FEMALE WIDOWHOOD
PER THOUSAND IN THE DECCAN, 1881[117]

	Under 15		15 and over	
	M	F	M	F
Deshasta brahman	2	12	130	371
Konkanastha brahman	1	7	103	338
Prabhu	3	3	85	317
Maratha-kunbi	2	8	73	288
Mali	2	7	70	257
Sonar	12	19	101	286
Sutar	3	9	72	233
Kasar	4	10	101	277
Kumbhar	5	11	82	257
Lohar	3	7	72	234
Mahar	3	8	62	259
Mang	3	9	73	234

What is striking about the figures in the table is their suggestion that if the numbers of widowed women relative to men are any guide, middle and lower caste practice by the 1880s did not actually differ fundamentally from that of the first three high caste groups in the table. The report itself repeated the usual view that 'the remarriage of widows is a practice confined to the lower and middle classes', but almost in the same breath pointed out that 'the large proportion of the widowed females is one of the main characteristics of the returns for the whole indigenous community'. It gave no overall explanation for the very large numbers of widowed Hindu women, merely noting that these were diffused over the whole age range, rather than being concentrated at the end of life as it was amongst the Muslims, and that although the famine in the southern part of the presidency in 1876–7 had pushed up the numbers of widows there, their ratio for the Deccan and Gujarat was actually very similar.[118]

It does seem, therefore, that possibilities for remarriage may have become increasingly restricted for quite a wide range of women over the course of the century. In part, this may have been a result of the way in which, as Lucy Carroll has argued, the

Widows' Remarriage Act of 1856, administered by brahman
lawyers and Victorian judges, tended to promote 'brahmanical
values which held widow remarriage in disrepute', by driving out
customary law, under which most widowed women had rights of
inheritance in their husband's estates, in favour of statutory and
brahmanical book law which disinherited them.[119] But it may also
have been associated with the same social processes that produced
the tighter and more Hinduized forms of purdah described above.
Like purdah, moreover, restrictions on remarriage could also be a
relatively cost-free means of enhancing family dignity, particularly
for those whose social aspirations outran their resources. Indeed,
such restrictions may actually have been an effective way of
protecting and adding to those resources. They removed the
danger that women might seek to partition the family estate, and
also enabled families to retain a widow's labour. Many nineteenth-
century observers reported that widows often did the heaviest and
dirtiest work about the home, such as grinding, while the Maratha
reformer, Vasant Lingoji Birze, admonished his caste fellows for
what he saw as their increasing reluctance to remarry their
widows:

> Those people who have fallen into brahman customs
> should rethink this. Because today, many brahmans
> openly do widow remarriage. So it is not very sensible
> to cherish the desire to do as those who call themselves
> brahmans do. We should never think that widowed
> women are very useful in doing housework, so they
> should stay at home.[120]

In rather different forms, these trends may have been present in
large peasant communities more widely in India. David Pocock has
noted that the patidars of Gujarat gave up remarrying their widows
towards the end of the nineteenth century, as prosperous kanbis
built a respectable 'patidar' status for themselves and sought new
marriage strategies to consolidate their dominance in rural society.
For the Jats of Haryana, Prem Chowdhry has described how
widows could remarry, but family pressure meant that a woman
almost always married one of her husband's younger brothers.
What the Jats lost in social status they regained in material terms,
since in practice Jat women's rights to their husband's estates were
seldom in danger of leaving the family.[121]

Set in this wider context, then, Tarabai's own insistence that restrictions on widowed women were not just a brahman problem becomes more explicable. What also seems to have goaded her, however, was the way in which widows were written about and discussed in public, particularly when they failed to live up to the impossible ideals of chastity prescribed for them. In particular, she mentions the case of the widow Vijaylakshmi referred to above. Vijaylakshmi's case may have been partly what she had in mind when she talked in her introduction of how

> everyday now people go about pinning the blame on women all the time, as if everything bad was their fault! When I saw this, my whole mind just began churning and shaking out of feeling for the honour of woman-kind. So I lost all my fear, I just couldn't stop myself writing about it in this very biting language. In fact, if I could have found even stronger words to describe how you men all stick together and cover up for each other I would have used them in my clumsy way. Because you men are all the same, all full of lies and dirty tricks.[122]

To conclude this section, it is worth just looking at a little of this public discussion. It covered a broad spectrum of opinion, from sympathy for Vijaylakshmi in view of the temptations to which the miserable lot of Hindu widows made them subject, to outraged demands that her unchaste life and monstrous crime receive the ultimate penalty. Conservative opinion was unambiguous. A correspondent to the *Shivaji* demanded to know why any mercy should be shown to this inhuman mother: widows, he said, ought to refrain from immoral lives, and if they abandoned themselves to vice they must take the consequences.[123] Tarabai herself mentions the *Pune Vaibhav*, which had evidently denounced Vijaylakshmi as an example of Indian womanhood corrupted from her *pativrata* by modern values.[124]

In many ways, however, liberal opinion actually shared the same set of assumptions. If for conservatives, women were wicked, for liberals they were morally weak. The Prarthana Samaj news-paper *Subodha Patrika* pointed out the temptations to vice and crime that widows were subject to, and urged that they should be educated as the means of avoiding them.[125] The *Bombay Samachar* agreed that the crime of infanticide was indeed a horrible one,

but urged that account should be taken of widows' peculiar circumstances, and a period of imprisonment instead of outright execution
used to deter women from wickedness.[126] This theme of imprisonment and shame as a deterrent to women was given wide publicity.
The well-known Maratha reformer and Diwan of Baroda State, Sir
T. Madhava Rao, published a long article in the *Times of India*. He
agreed that capital punishment was too extreme; a long term of
imprisonment would be a much better deterrent because it would
actually be a much harsher punishment to the woman than hanging,
in which 'the woman is released from all pain in five minutes'.

> Imprisonment would punish the woman by making her
> suffer that pain—that very pain which she most dreaded.
> Sentence her publicly, send her to gaol publicly, keep
> her there publicly, and let her suffer the pain of shame
> which she had dreaded so much. Would not that be a
> sufficiently deterring punishment?

It would also be a much better deterrent. For women in India
seldom went to see executions, and most of them were unable to
read about them in the newspapers.

> But in the case of the punishment I advocate, the female
> culprit being alive in gaol, is likely to be seen, especially
> if sentenced to labour. Being kept alive, she is frequently
> the subject of conversation, and consequently her punish
> ment is kept more before the female public mind.[127]

This, then, was liberal logic carried to its conclusion. Infanticide
was still basically the women's fault, but because this fault sprang
from weakness, women should not actually be hanged, but
punished and made an example of to encourage others to resist
temptation. In his summing up, the judge, Mr Justice West, added
his own view that women deserved no clemency at all when, as in
this case, 'the ordinary associations which clustered around the
ideal of a woman were entirely perverted':

> The woman who herself disregarded the proper func
> tions of her sex was in an especial degree disqualified
> from claiming the kindness and consideration which we
> ordinarily accord to the sex, because of their having
> feelings which this woman had thrown aside.[128]

It is not clear exactly what of this Tarabai might have read apart
from the *Pune Vaibhav*, although the themes of female vice and
weakness are common enough. It is not difficult to see why she
should have been angered by it, or have felt that 'when a woman
like Vijaylakshmi goes wrong, every woman gets included in the
blame'.[129] While restrictions on remarriage were getting tighter,
and liberal reformers talked impotently from the sidelines, widows
like Vijaylakshmi found themselves in an impossible position:
urged to impossible ideals of *pativrata*, condemned from either side
when they failed, and all this in circumstances which made it very
hard for them to answer back.

There were other areas too where Tarabai was concerned with
pativrata as an increasingly popular model for women's behaviour.
She also saw it running through much of the new Marathi print
culture, with far-reaching consequences for the more general ways
in which women were talked about and represented in nineteenth
century society. We turn now to examine these aspects of her
argument and their context.

PATIVRATAS AND WHORES:
WOMEN IN POPULAR LITERATURE

Historians have long appreciated the extent to which later
nineteenth century vernacular literatures were important
vehicles for a range of religious and regional political
identities. It is only more recently that we have begun to discover
their significance in the construction of gender identities.[130]
Tarabai's text is illuminating here, for in it we have the views of a
woman actually reading and seeing some of the new vernacular
print genres taking shape, and not in the least liking what she sees.
For what dominated many of them was a peculiar mixture of
adulation for an idealized *pativrata*, titillating descriptions of
suffering womanly virtue under seige, and scandalized accounts of
'independent' loose women and whores. As we shall see, this
popular and commercially very successful genre reflected very
much the blending of Victorian and brahmanic values that elsewhere shaped some of the new models for respectable Hindu

womanhood. Here, too, we have the same combination of veneration for wifely purity and revilement for women who showed any
evidence of independent sexuality, as a sure sign of women gone
wrong. This literature seems to have reinforced Tarabai's sense of
contradiction and impossibility for women in this emerging Hindu
culture: made as they were into a symbol for all sorts of traditions
and institutions over which they had little control, alternatively
encouraged towards impossible models of wifely devotion and held
as the innate sources of moral weakness behind all social evil,
constantly discussed but without a public voice of their own.

Like other Indian vernaculars, Marathi literature was before
the coming of print at the end of the eighteenth century dominated
by verse forms, in the shape of versions of and commentaries on
the great classics of Sanskrit literature, as well as a rich and
flourishing tradition of devotional poetry associated with the *bhakti*
tradition. From the 1820s and 1830s, print literature and the use of
prose expanded together, and with patronage from missionaries,
the Bombay government and a range of private societies, Marathi
writers brought out translations of the Bible and of Persian, Sanskrit
and English tales: *Aesop's Fables*, the *Arabian Nights*, the Sanskrit
Panchatantra, Robinson Crusoe, Ivanhoe, Lamb's *Tales from Shakes-*
peare, as well as a range of Victorianized homilies intended for the
instruction and improvement of readers.[131] From mid-century,
however, many Marathi writers began to give their work a rather
sharper moral point, in the collections of tales, short stories and
little sketches from which emerged the first Marathi novels and
plays of the 1860s. Most strikingly, though, they were dominated
by themes and stories about women, as the editors of the *Dnya-*
nodaya and *Dnyanprakash* newspapers agreed in the course of one
of their exchanges about the worth of this new genre in 1864.[132]

Typically, these were highly-coloured romances, featuring racy
and explicit fantasies of women's virtue in danger and the shocking
vices of the fallen. They drew clearly on a variety of earlier
literatures: on tales like the *Arabian Nights* for their adventure
element, on the mildly pornographic tradition of Sanskrit stories
for their accounts of lusty young men's adventures, on the highly
moralizing dramas about virtue in danger that were popular in
contemporary Victorian literature, and on the strong themes of
pativrata and womanly chastity that pervaded brahmanic religious
culture. The result was an extremely ambiguous blend of fantasy,

voyeurism and stern injuctions about the consequences of womanly weakness. Tarabai describes some of these stories and plays in detail: *Muktamala*, published in 1861, *Manjughosha*, in 1868; the play *Manorama*, published in 1871, and a virtual genre in itself of *Stricharitra*, 'Lives of Women', that were published from the 1850s onwards. All of these were extremely popular. *Stricharitra* was on to its third part by 1862, and spawned more imitations: *Vidagdha stricharitra*, 'Lives of Clever Women', in 1871, and *Sushikshit stricharitra*, 'Lives of Educated Women' in 1872. *Muktamala* was into its fifth edition by 1880; *Manjughosha* was in its third by 1874 and *Manorama* was in its second by 1877. There were many others in the same genre, and they appear to have enjoyed considerable commercial success.[133]

There were a range of *Stricharitra*, and it is not quite clear which one exactly Tarabai refers to, though their themes were fairly consistent. First published was that of Ramjee Gunnojee, a retired hospital assistant, referred to as 'Doctorsahib' throughout the book, who warned in his preface that he had got a special *sanad* or warrant from the Calcutta government to stop anyone from pirating his book.[134] Its full English title was

> Streechuritra or Female Narration, comprizing their course of life, BEHAVIOUR, and undertaking in four parts with Moral reprimands checking Obscenity to secure Chastity.[135]

The stories in the book are based round the nightly meetings of the 'Doctor' with the young girl Pritai, when he tells her tales of virtue always on the brink of corruption, and the terrible fate of wives who are 'hard-hearted, cunning and wicked'.[136] The 'Doctor' finished each of them with a *tatparaya* or moral, like the following:

> Such is the love of adulterous women. Because the woman who deserts her home and wedded husband loses all her fear and behaves just as she likes. Through that, she gets into great difficulties. So, Pritai, you should not be like that. Woman's minds are very fickle, and so when the fortitude of their minds is undone, they have no fear of the worst courses of action.[137]

Often, the concern with womanly unchastity was hardly even a veneer for what were actually pornographic tales. The stories in

Chintaman Dixit Joshi's *Vidagdha Stri Charitra* might well have been those that Tarabai described as 'so nasty and disgusting you feel ashamed just reading them'.[138] They moralize about 'clever' women really just as a frame for a collection of Decameron-like tales about the amorous adventures of two young men with a series of wildly lustful and gratefully submissive women who are prepared to go to any lengths to deceive their husbands. More commonly, though, the element of moralizing about *pativrata* in its updated form dominated. The reformer, Govind Vinayak Kanitkar's *Sushikshit Stricharitra*, aimed at showing 'the meaning of the word pativrata, and its glory', dealt directly with questions of women's virtue, and how far they could have education and independence without endangering it.[139] Far from ruining *pativrata* and making women idle and insubordinate as many traditionalists thought, Kanitkar urged that education was in fact the best guarantee of womanly chastity and enlightened respectability in mothers and daughters alike. We are led into this through the adventures of the virtuous princess Chandraseniya, whose experiences lead her to admonish readers that

> So women, bearing all these reasons in mind, should never ever allow the desire for a man other than their husbands to enter their minds. Because in this matter, men's affairs are one thing and women's quite another. Women do not have the same independence given them as do men. Women absolutely have to remain a part of the man's body. If women start to wish for the same independence as is given to men, great disasters will follow.[140]

The best way of avoiding this was actually the right kind of education for women. Chandraseniya's mother was a fine example of 'how much an educated woman takes care that her daughter remains in a good state':

> So that she should not turn out mischievous, she taught her to behave with restraint. She never even let filthy language, and the words of naughty jokes fall upon her ears ... averting the face modestly before men, keeping the eyes lowered, protecting her modesty, being shy, behaving humbly, not speaking any bad words, not

letting bad ideas come into her mind, not chatting idly
here and there, reading religious books, teaching her
morals—the mother and father held to the course of
guiding her along such a good path. And so in this way,
the chances of daughters turning out bad is very
small.[141]

For these reasons, Kanitkar urged, 'women should at all times and
always stay true to their *pativrata dharma*. There is no clothing, no
jewels, nothing that so ornaments a woman as her loyalty to
pativrata'.[142] With impossible models of womanly purity like these,
we can well understand Tarabai's furious demand to know 'how
much truth there is in all these stories? You can look as hard as you
like for some real-life examples, but you won't find any'.[143]

This peculiar mixture of romantic fantasy, titillation and
concern with updated forms of *pativrata* ran through all of the
works that Tarabai discusses. *Manjughosha*, by Naro Sadashiv
Risbud, a head clerk in the Public Works Department in Sholapur,
is interesting because it is clearly where Tarabai encountered the
verses about women's evil natures from the old Sanskrit poem the
Bhartrhari, which she quotes earlier in her book.[144] Risbud puts the
words into the mouth of the outraged raja of the story, who has just
been told that his daughter has been sneaking out of the palace to
meet her lover, and is probably several months pregnant already:

See, however much a man may be thoughtful, wise and
a lion in bravery, once he falls into the clutches of such
an enticing and bold woman, he becomes at once soft
and cowed. There is a very good sloka of Bhartrhari
describing this.[145]

This, with Tarabai's equally misogynistic extract from Shridhar's
popular Marathi *Ramavijaya*, is the subject of her elaborate
rebuttal over the second half of the book.[146]

Here, then, we have older brahmanic constructions of feminine
nature feeding through directly into colonial print culture, and
blending very comfortably with its more Victorian themes. Against
these, Tarabai demanded of her male readers: 'Why do you cry
so much about pativrata dharma, when it's you men that scheme
and ruin homes and families?'[147] We can also see why she felt so
strongly that such stories actually tainted all women with the

same stain of moral weakness and vice, including the very mothers
and daughters of men like Risbud who wrote this nonsense:

> These are all women too, aren't they? Or are these all
> different, all from a different species of women? If you
> talk about women, you have to talk about them all. You
> say that women are like axes, vessels of all cunning,
> market-places for wickedness, wreckers of the path to
> heaven? But if you hand out names like that to women,
> what names should we call you? Mother-haters? Slan-
> derers of your own mothers?[148]

The play *Mānorama* is perhaps the most extreme combination
of misogynism, voyeuristic detail and heavy-handed moralizing.
Published in 1871 by Mahadev Balkrishna Chitale, a Senior
Student in Deccan College, Poona, it was not a romance at all, but
the first of what were to be many plays and short stories dealing
with the 'social problems' of abortion, infanticide and prostitution
said to be associated with early marriage and the denial of rights to
remarriage. *Manorama* treads an extremely thin line between
sensationalism and 'serious' reformist concern, with Chitale himself defending the play as only a mirror held up to nature.[149] The
stories in the book were certainly explicit. We have drunken scenes
from a Karachi brothel, where the inmates explain how they have
run away from bad homes and husbands, and knowing widow prostitutes persuade younger women of the attractions of freedom.[150]
There is a melodramatic episode in which a brahman widow
apprehended with a dead baby in her arms is led away by sepoys,
to confess to the police inspector how the local prostitutes helped
her to get medicine to induce an abortion.[151] Then there are the
inevitable scenes concerning *pativrata*, such as when the adulterous
wife boasts of her virtue only to be unmasked by her lover, who
stands up and says he knows she has two moles on her right thigh,
and holds up the ring she gave him the previous night 'in the throes
of passionate love'.[152] Concern for the plight of widows is certainly
the overt theme of the play, but its main attraction looks likely to
have been its highly spiced detail. As Tarabai retorts to Chitale's
plea that his purpose was serious moral instruction, 'what I want to
say to you, Mr Author, is—don't even dream of pretending that the
story will frighten men and women so much they'll never do it
again'.[153]

To refute such representations of women, Tarabai also tried to bring out what she felt to be the the real social pressures shaping women's behaviour. She depicts the successful man, impatient for a smart new bride and caring no more about his old wife than he would 'the alley or cowshed at the back of the house'.[154] She talks of an ordinary wife's burden of heavy domestic labour, and her particular anxieties—wanting a son, wanting her husband's affection, her chilling fear of widowhood when he became ill.[155] She discusses the plight of women lured from their homes by lovers who promise them everything, and then desert them to infanticide or a life of prostitution. While she voices strong disapproval of adultery and sexual licence, she makes it clear that she is not, like many of her more conventional contemporaries, just attacking prostitutes and 'immoral women' themselves. Prostitution was not a symptom of women's natural propensity for vice but rather a social phenomenon for which men were largely responsible. There was no 'nest somewhere, that all prostitutes come out of': rather, they were women who had been lured or turned out of their homes by men, and now they engaged in it because 'it's just the way they earn their living, and if they don't do what their customers tell them, next day they go hungry'.[156]

It is worth noting that Tarabai was by no means the first to attack these new genres of literature and their lurid depictions of women. There was a prolonged newspaper debate in 1865 on these emerging Marathi novels and plays, and in particular on the question of how far their ostensible 'social' concern with women was actually for serious moral purposes. A correspondent to the *Dnyanodaya* affirmed that there were

> many people who will take up such shameful work for
> the sake of money, and people who put on plays are
> among them. These plays started up ten or twelve years
> back, and because they have been supported by some
> learned and senior gentlemen in Bombay, they have
> spread very much.

The writer described how he had gone unsuspectingly to one such play as a schoolboy, but it had been full of foul language, and its audience, while containing a few educated men, were mainly 'just people who pretended to be learned, and illiterate dolts'.[157] Another correspondent ascribed the spread of plays in particular to their great commercial potential, as people saw how companies attracted audiences and the support of local magnates:

> The Poona Hindu players made a huge amount of money from their work, and also got a lot of support from educated people. So, seeing this, Nagar people's mouths began to water, and they took up the same work themselves. So the Poona Hindu players took the so-called foundations of reform to Nagar. Not content with that, these reformers of the country have even moved to graze the rich pastures of Rahuri: I never even dreamed that they would favour Rahuri! As in Nagar, there also the munsif, mamledar and other important people gave their support, and so the work is going on well in this place also. The performers earn a lot of money, and the people of Majkur town, seeing that such very important gentlemen were all in favour, began also to learn the work. And also, some people wanted to come and see the play but could not or did not want to pay the money. So our charitable bigwigs here said that even without money people ought to come and see this fine performance, and paid with their own money to invite anyone to come who wanted to![158]

The early literary critic K. B. Marathe was also very disdainful, lamenting that it was impossible even to buy any of the old Maratha histories now, while two editions of *Muktamala* and *Manjughosha* had gone through in a year.

> In each novel, there are tremendous assaults on the pativrata of women. At every turn, there are such difficulties that it seems as though pativrata must be ruined. It seems utterly impossible that these women's pativrata should remain unstained through these diffi-culties. The women who remain pure through these trials of their pativrata are not of this world.[159]

Not only did these works lack any coherent plot or sense of who were the main protagonists, but their focus on drunkenness, prostitution and adultery were not calculated to instil moral purity into anyone. 'Even men will feel sorrow to hear such descriptions of women; is it any wonder that women will loathe them?

Respectable women will tear up these books and throw them on the fire.'[160]

How, then, can we understand the evident popular appeal and commercial success of books and plays on these themes? Between them, these two genres would have spanned a wide range of audiences. Those for the books, whilst relatively narrow in social terms, were clearly voracious consumers, and would probably have come from backgrounds similar to those of their authors: provincial officials like Risbud, lesser professional people like the hospital assistant Ramjee Gunnojee, college students like Chitale. These were people who had literacy, money and leisure enough to read, whose wealth derived in large part from state employment, and for whom these new print genres represented an important means of participating in its wider culture. Audiences for the plays were clearly wider, including, as the *Dnyanodaya* correspondents suggested, local magnates who were their patrons, some educated, and large numbers of local people with little or no literate skills. With its images of chastity, suffering and deference, and its lurid accounts of positive female sexuality punished, this new literature held out what seems to have been a very attractive blend of racy detail, prurient moral earnestness and social conservatism.

There is a further and final dimension to this new writing, which may have lent Tarabai's fury a sharper edge. For these authors and audiences were also in the process of shaping and creating Marathi as a print language suitable for prose and dramatic literature, as were their counterparts in other parts of India at the same time. In his introduction to *Muktamala*, Laxman Moreshvar Halbe said that it was his aim as an author to develop people's interest in Marathi as a language suitable for prose writing.[161] At another level, the same was true for Marathi newspapers. It is possible to see the same sense of having to invent a new language, 'a new terminology to make our writings effective' in Tilak's reminiscences about early difficulties with the *Kesari* newspaper.[162] In a range of different fields, such writers were consciously exploring and actively promoting Marathi as a print language and powerful new means of communication and representation. And as Tarabai saw it, this new medium was not only being monopolized by men, but employed in a particularly damaging way against women. Hence, perhaps, her furious accusation:

With you, you don't use the knowledge you have in
your own bodies. You roam around from one place to
the next, looking through all sorts of books. You get so
full of learning you can play any part you please, get
yourself out of difficulty—it all comes so easy to you.
But these poor women, always shut in the house—what
knowledge can they have, except of what's between the
stove and the doorstep?[163]

This brings us to wider questions of politics and power as they
appear in Tarabai's writing.

GENDER AND POLITICS IN COLONIAL SOCIETY

Like her male contemporaries in the Satyashodhak Samaj,
Tarabai saw colonial rule as a source of many benefits for
women. Under the British, they had 'the gift of education
and their minds made strong enough to face all sorts of mental and
practical circumstances with courage'.[164] In other ways, however, a
deeper sense of regret pervades her text for what she sees as the
ruin of the country at the hands of men who flocked to the culture
of the rulers even as they tried to lock women out from any of its
benefits and to cut back on their freedoms. The Maratha circles to
which she belonged had a very strong historical sense, particularly
of the progressive loss of their power and status as warrior-
landholders within a colonial culture seemingly now dominated by
brahman administrators and professionals. What is interesting is
that Tarabai has her own clear sense of a vanished Indian warrior
and courtly culture, where some women at least had commanded
power and wealth on their own terms. This had been a culture of
magnificent consumption, where women were indispensable to the
status and honour of the court, where queens lived in luxury and
enjoyed a measure of sexual freedom while their men were away campaigning, and where women had some means of asserting themselves:

People in those days used to yield to three kinds of will:
of women, of children, and of kings. But in today's
circumstances there's only one, and that's rulers.
Children can still be wilful about things too. But women

can't get their way any more, I don't see how they can.
If any of them tries she loses the skin off her back with a
beating, a ration enough to make her remember it for
six months or more. This is what happens when women
try being wilful now.[165]

But all this was now gone, as men under the new regime became
penpushers instead of warriors and scrambled to take on the rulers'
culture, with such damaging consequences, as she saw it, for
women. This was one of the things, she explained, that had pushed
her into writing:

I'm doing it to make you men open your eyes and take a
new look at your country and have some pride in it,
rather than each one of you just abandoning the
dharma, habits and customs of his own country. I'm
doing it out of the hope that you might stop treating all
women as though they had committed a crime and
making their lives a hell for it.[166]

What, then, are we to make of Tarabai's pervasive feeling of
regret at the disappearance of India's old royal and military
cultures, and of particular disadvantage for women in colonial
society? In some ways, her views may well have had a powerful
logic of their own. Almost all recent studies of India during the
eighteenth century have emphasized the fluidity of its politics and
the openness of its state systems to men with appropriate military,
political or entrepreneurial skills.[167] There has been rather less
discussion of the extent to which this was also a congenial political
milieu for ambitious and independent women at many different
levels of society. As we have seen above, many ordinary women
went on campaign with their husbands without being secluded,
and enjoyed a considerable degree of freedom in the camps. As
many eighteenth-century observers noted, royal courts as well as
armies provided opportunities of patronage and support for a wide
range of women.[168] At the level of high politics in particular,
women had remarkably good access to state power. Neither Indo-
Muslim nor Hindu rules for succession, as they were applied in the
eighteenth century, assumed any automatic right for eldest sons.
Rather, as Bayly has described, rivals for power emerged from the
complex of ties of blood, affection and power within the *zenana*,

and a successful contender established his authority and legitimacy in the process of beating off competition itself and thereafter of ruling with an appropriate combination of authoritarian ruthlessness and incorporative skills.[169] Aristocratic women were not only particularly well placed to influence these processes; they could themselves assume power as regents or widows if they had ambition and the right qualities. Moreover, marriage ties assumed a particular importance in late pre-colonial India. In the building up of many new rulerships, these were often a more powerful means of consolidating alliances and incorporating key groups such as financiers, military entrepreneurs, centres of religious power and the like, than clientship alone. In many eighteenth century states, a dense network of marriage ties linked royal with banking and military families, and this also placed women in strategic positions.[170]

In western India certainly, women could and did pursue these opportunities in the shifting alliances of eighteenth century politics. Women such as Tarabai Bhosle, Ahalyabai Holkar and Tulsabai Holkar all ruled for long periods as widows or regents.[171] The three widows of Mahadji Shinde went to war against his adopted son for a larger share of his estate, supported by his alienated brahman servants, and were themselves on campaign for long periods at a time.[172] The brahman women Anandibai and Gopikabai, while not direct contenders for power themselves, exercised in different ways a profound influence on the political strategies of their menfolk.[173] Others deputized for absent husbands, such as the wife of Hiroo Nand, minister to the Maratha chief Fatehsingh Rao Gaekwad of Baroda, and others again were active as diplomats on their husband's accounts within the wider political system, such as Lakshmibai, wife of the Kolhapur chief Khem Savant, who obtained for her husband titles and emblems of royalty from the Mughal emperor, or Dipamba of Tanjore, who arranged conciliation between Ekoji and Shivaji Bhosle early in the century.[174] Questions of caste and social practice were another arena in which women were extremely active, fighting as Dipamba did in Tanjore or Gopikabai did in Poona to maintain and improve the purity of caste practice.[175] Women were also able to enhance their power by forming sexual relationships with ministers or pretending to do so.[176] Whatever formal seclusion there was in the *zenana*, then, it did not cut women like these off from politics, but rather the opposite. The half-humorous references of nineteenth century observers like Sleeman to 'domination from behind the curtain' may actually have reflected what was once a serious historical reality.[177]

Early Company governments like Elphinstone's in Bombay were naturally anxious to recruit a range of influential and skilled groups into the colonial administration: brahmans for their scribal skills and presumed religious authority, princely rulers like the old Maratha raja of Satara to undercut the authority of the defeated regime of the peshwas. Women powerholders found, of course, no corresponding role.[178] This was not because they lacked political, administrative, or scribal skills; as we have seen, women with these skills were by no means unusual. Nor were women seen as a source of expertise in early social reform debates such as that over *sati* even though women in pre-colonial India had been active in such matters, and most of these issues concerned women directly. What is remarkable, indeed, in the long stretch of social reform debate and consultation from the question of *sati* onwards, is how completely 'Indian opinion' came to mean masculine opinion, for colonial administrators and Indian reformers, nationalists and conservatives alike. As for those women who were left in positions of political power in the Indian states not yet absorbed into Company territory, they appear in the records now only as a succession of obstinate old dowagers or intriguing regents who have somehow to be got rid of for their feminine incompetence or sexual misdemeanours.[179] Later in the century indeed, colonial officials found a more effective way to sever the links that remained in Indian states between court women and the exercise of political power, by transferring young princes and future rulers into the closely supervised and masculine world of the new Indian public schools. In 1844, Sleeman complained that in India 'there are no universities or public schools in which young men might escape, as they do in Europe, from the enervating and stultifying influence of the zenana'. By 1893, his editor Vincent Smith could congratulate himself that this was no longer the case, although as he noted, 'the influence of the zenana is invariably directed against every proposal to remove a young nobleman from home for the purpose of education'.[180]

Therefore, if there were many areas in which the Company's government and the Indian elite sought to preserve 'tradition', women's participation in politics was certainly not one of them. Rather, the nineteenth century saw the gradual removal of women, except as tokens and figures in exchanges between men, from what came to be the more exclusively masculine 'public' world of politics and administration, social reform debate and early nationalist organizing. According to this model, as we have seen, respectable women's proper sphere was now home and domestic life, and the public models for their behaviour variants on the themes of devoted wife and enlightened motherhood. In this context, it is ironic, indeed, that so many reformers and nationalists turned to the image of the 'ancient freedoms' of Aryan women when they wished to provide 'indigenous' examples of powerful and respected women. Eighteenth century history might have furnished examples much closer to home.

Much more difficult to explain, of course, is the place of these complex social changes in the construction of colonial hegemony. As I have argued elsewhere, however, it may be significant that on these issues at least, colonial officials and key groups of elite Indian men came to share very similar language and preconceptions about the significance of women and their proper sphere and duties.[181] For both, debates about the moral worth of cultures and traditions were most appropriately conducted as it were at second-hand, around the objectified figure of woman, whose domain of family, custom and religion both sides agreed to be outside the normal realm of politics and the state. Partha Chatterjee has seen these emerging divisions between public and private, politics and the purely 'social' domains of family, custom and religion, as an effective way of resisting colonial intervention, driven by 'the refusal of nationalism to make the women's question an issue of political negotiation with the colonial state'.[182] On another reading, though, it may well have been that just the reverse was true. For what is striking is actually the broad degree of consensus between Indian politicians and the colonial state, established early in the nineteenth century, and reinforced in the years after the wars of 1857, that for all routine civil purposes domestic and family questions were outside the purview of the state, except in so far as it was necessary to 'administer' the appropriate community and religious law. There were, of course, occasions where Indian governments did legislate, as in the abolition of *sati* in 1829, the Widows' Remarriage Act of 1856, or most controversially in legislating to raise the age of consent in 1891. Even these interventions, however, were in practice extremely limited in their social effects, and made with extreme reluctance, often after prolonged campaigning by non-official groups. Certainly, there was no general colonial project actively to 'modernize' and transform Indian society. This, indeed, was precisely the problem from the perspective of someone like Tarabai, and for other politically active people outside nationalist circles who continued to look to the colonial state for such a radical role, and were continually disappointed.

If domestic public distinctions were more an area of broad agreement than one where nationalists thwarted and resisted the colonial state, the same distinctions also served to extend the authority of Indian men at many different levels—caste and family heads, social reformers and conservatives, politicians and lawyers— over their own womenfolk, and at a time when such control had taken on a new importance for a range of social and caste rivalries. There were now a much wider range of fields and issues in which women had no recourse to the state, or had recourse only under the rubric of a separate 'religious' law that was itself being defined very much in a brahman image. It was precisely such questions of men's power over women that were at stake when, for example, the conservative Bombay lawyer V. N. Mandlik opposed legislation in the 1884 enquiry on the grounds that it would 'introduce a system of state interference with the most cherished objects of Hindu domestic life'.[183]

It is in this broad context that Tarabai's critique of the politics of gender in colonial society is best understood. As she sees it, men had gained access to a new range of powers under colonial rule, which they used for their own vanity and self-aggrandizement, even as they tried to shut women out from its benefits and lock them into an ossified religious culture for which men themselves now had no regard. She looks at dress, food, travel, new forms of consumption, employment and education that Indian men embraced so enthusiastically, from boots and stockings to pigeon and liquor for supper, from travel by steamship to living in colonial-style bungalows, a rush to embrace British fashions that only made men a laughing stock. Yet many of the same men had the effrontery to put themselves forward as the champions of an inviolate religious tradition at home:

> You keep on trying to be just like them, yet you go on about them not putting their hands in our religion! But how much of this religion is there left now? You go

wherever you like in trains and boats, you dress just like
them—a jacket on your back, a hat on your head,
trousers, socks and shoes, a little handkerchief sprinkled
with lavender water in your hand, a pipe in your mouth
to finish it off. You turn yourselves into real live
sahibs...then you turn round and claim you're great
defenders of dharma! Aren't you even a bit ashamed
saying it?[184]

Reformers who pretended to want to do something were no better.
Men were 'full of talk' about reform,

but who actually does anything? You hold these great
meetings, you turn up at them in your fancy shawls and
embroidered turbans, you go through a whole ton of
supari nut, cartloads of betel leaves, you hand out all
sorts of garlands, you use up a tankful of rosewater,
then you come home. And that's it. That's all you do.
These phoney reform societies of yours have been around
for thirty, thirty-five years. What's the use of them?
You're all there patting yourselves on the back, but if
we look closely, they're about as much use as a spare tit
on a goat.[185]

Far from seeing the home and family as some sacrosanct domain,
she positively demanded state intervention to make it easier for
women to live and marry independently, and to punish men who
corrupted the innocent. For, as she says, 'If they don't reach in and
change this religion of ours, make women who are weak strong and
rescue them from this sham dharma and all the misery it makes—if
they don't, who will?'[186]

DIGNITY AND RESISTANCE:
WOMEN'S SUBCULTURES IN COLONIAL SOCIETY

If Tarabai was so savage in her criticism of the way that men
depicted women and excluded them from power, what
positive ideas of her own did she have about women's real
natures and proper rights and freedoms? The wide range of ways
in which she herself describes and represents women, contrasting
strongly with the impoverished stereotypes of contemporary

masculine discourse, is the most striking aspect of her text. Her
voice itself moves from urbane social commentary to the scathing
female abuse of the market-place, from mocking descriptions of
men's sexual pretensions to the pleas of a pious wife for domestic
harmony and companionship. We begin with her worldly-wise
picture of a 'real' woman at home with her husband, determinedly
refusing to be disturbed while she has her tea, swearing over the
cooking, and refusing to relax with her husband after dinner with
some *pan*. From there we move to a celebration of women's very
real power and importance, as opposed to the insults and belittle-
ment common in contemporary public culture: women as a source
of power and pleasure in the world, 'even more piercing than
money', women as auspicious wives so much more esteemed than
'a stray solitary man on his own', women whose bright glances
could reduce men to helplessness, women whose sexual appeal was
like 'a blazing ball of fire', women who were devoted wives and
loving mothers, whose 'soft minds' were so easily deceived only
because 'God has weighed them down with all life's burdens'. But
then there are free women with bayonets in their hands more
ferocious even than the warrior queen of Jhansi, women who curse
and spit at the very names of lovers who have left them, women
who disdainfully reject inferior husbands or brazenly set up with
other women as prostitutes in order to survive. Finally, it is to
women that Adimaya, the source of all generative power in the
universe, has given 'a fickle strength' like her own.

> And it was her she set to drive on this cart of worldly
> life. You men have only one thing to do and that's fill
> up the cart. It's in her hands to look after it and drive it
> forward. This is one power womankind has.[187]

Besides this, she demands of her male readers: 'Who cares about a
vagabond like you? Neither child nor little lad. You might as well
lay down your head under a tree, it makes no difference to any
one.' It was because of this special place in the world that people
called women Lakshmi, goddess of fortune and source of all
auspicious grace, who created a splendid temple wherever she
made her home.[188] Indeed, right at the end of the text, and in
strong contrast with much of her earlier language and imagery, she
makes a plea for a genuine and benevolent *pativrata*. This was not
the absurd idealized self-abnegation that journalists and politicians,

priests and novelists talked about, but a kind of public dignity and respect for women through which they should all be able to be virtuous and respected wives in happy homes, 'beloved by all and their foreheads filled with the auspicious marks of marriage'.[189]

It is clear then, that she was not arguing from abstract or 'modern' principles of rights or equality, except at the most commonsense level. Nor, indeed, does she draw at all on themes from devotional religion, through which as we saw above, some women in pre-colonial society expressed their dissent from brahmanical religious culture. For her what seems to have mattered was not merely a religious milieu in which women could find acceptance as equals, but much more concrete changes in the domestic and social circumstances of women. What, then, were the sources of her arguments and ideas about women? Some, like her nostalgia for aspects of pre-colonial Indian culture, may have been part of her Maratha social milieu, given an extra edge by her own position on its political margins. In other and contradictory ways, she was clearly caught up in and drawn to a political culture which saw the colonial state as a potential agent of social change, laying the basis for a new kind of educated and self-respecting womanhood for whom the original ideals of *pativrata*, observed by men and women alike, would still provide a basis for dignity and mutuality in marriage.

Other themes about the honour and worth of women may reflect a wider contemporary female culture. Sometimes, of course, this is difficult to say with certainty: images of woman as Lakshmi and as Adimaya, for example, are shared at many levels in Hindu religious culture.[190] It is more difficult to know how far her own reading of these images, which confers on women such absolute superiority over men reduced to mere servants and vagabonds, would have been a common one. Other themes, however, are more clearly traceable. Her images of women as ferocious warriors with a fiery sexuality is strongly reminiscent of the fierce female power divinities that Susan Bayly has described in eighteenth century south India religious culture ourside the narrow circles of brahmanic precept and practice.[191] Very many of her themes are echoed in women's oral tradition, certainly if the collections of Marathi women's songs that were made in the 1940s are any guide. These songs, sung mostly as women sat grinding corn together in the early mornings, express many of the sentiments and images of everyday life and the very practical concern for women that emerge in her writing. These songs talk of the tender love of wives, mothers and sisters compared with men's inconstancy and hardness of heart, the hardships of daughters-in-law who toil like hired bullocks, the misery of wives given to unsuitable husbands like cows to the butcher, the wickedness of fathers who give their daughters to old men or to men already married, the love and freedom that women find when they return to their mother's homes, and women's proud tradition of chastity compared to the selfish pleasures of men. Many of the stories and characters of Hindu mythology that Tarabai invokes and plays with so easily also appeared in women's songs.[192]

There is also much evidence to suggest that what she says belongs squarely to a subculture of 'respectable' widowed and other women living outside conventional family structures, who were prepared to defy caste and brahmanic convention to help each other or themselves to maintain some kind of dignity and independence. A correspondent to the *Dnyanprakash* newspaper in 1855, for example, reported about a woman in Satara district:

> In Padali village of Taragava peta, a man called Dada Purohit forcibly cut off the hair of his young widowed sister, against her will, and then he came to carry off her household property. But that learned widow wrote out a plea with her own hand and sent it in to the town, and her brother was taken away and put in prison. Our readers will be able to judge from this story what feats women can do who are clever at writing and the like.[193]

Women often acted together. In 1860, the Khatri newspaper *Vichardarpan* described how a meeting had been convened by some 'respectable and thoughtful gentlemen' of the caste to establish a caste association to bring about reform amongst its members. But on the very day appointed for the association's new rules to come into force, disaster struck:

> At that critical moment as fate would have it, the woman Sakhi, who had been boycotted from the caste and was residing pregnant at the house of her sister Bhivari and been brought to bed, was found to have been performing her Shashti puja and other such corrupted rituals.

The gentlemen of the caste had been aghast at such impropriety, and, feeling that the behaviour of the two women was not to be borne, brought a petition to the caste heads against the two sisters.[194] Sometimes, women were able to act with a remarkable degree of independence because of the support of their own parents. In 1883, a disturbed correspondent to the *Indu Prakash* newspaper reported a brahman woman who had left her husband to live with her father, and who was now planning to marry her two daughters without even consulting her husband. The correspondent demanded to know

> if she brings the marriage off, will it be according to the shastras, or what? And if it happens without her husband's permission, then with whose permission does it happen? So I hope that someone will find out a shastra that forbids it, and publish it in your newspaper.[195]

The Government of India's 1884 survey on widow remarriage reported a range of women who clearly shared Tarabai's views, and some even who wrote as she did. Gurshidapa Virbasapa, Deputy District Collector of Belgaum, reported that

> There is at present a brahman lady in Nasik, the wife of a deceased first class mamlatdar. She has not shaved herself on grounds that she does not want her body to be touched by another man. Her conduct is a model of morality. She has composed an essay to the effect, 1stly, that it is cruel on the part of men to disfigure women because their husbands happen to die; and 2ndly, that it is shameful to a spirited Hindu who secludes his wife from society simply to keep her off the evil eyes of bad men to allow his female relatives to be handled by the barbers.[196]

Pandit Narayan Kesow Vaidya reported that the widows of Surat, 'a most conservative district' were agitating for reform and had lodged a petition with the town authorities to introduce change.[197] There is also evidence from a much later period, in 1911, when women in the Poona Widows and Orphans Home were asked to write down their experiences. These again make points and use images that are strikingly similar to those Tarabai uses. 'KM', for

example, began by demanding to know whether all the myths were
true about the fate in hell of men whose wives refused to shave
their heads:

> But who had discovered that the husband of a widow is
> thrown into a pit of nightsoil unless she is shaved? Who
> will guarantee that all shaved widows remain moral?
> Every village has its outcastes. A woman with pure
> thoughts needs no such protection. Note the proverb,
> 'Outwardly painted face often carries a tainted heart'. A
> widow is not allowed to speak to a male stranger, but
> she is forced to go alone into a closed room to get
> herself shaved by a low class barber! Bravo! Such
> relations, bravo! ... Why is a widow treated so harshly?
> She has not killed her husband. She never even brooked
> the idea![198]

Widows who were 'independent' and, even worse, refused to
shave their heads, were also the subject of a number of extremely
hostile plays, again combining the themes of purity and prostitution that we have seen above: *Svairasvakesha*, 'Wanton widows
who keep their hair', or D. V. Joglekar's highly salacious play,
Independent Widows and Their Youthful Daughters, which depicted
brahman widows running a public eating house that doubled as a
brothel.[199] This is interesting, because a number of sources from the
1860s describe how high-caste widowed women with no other
means of support used to set up eating houses, something they
could do since their caste status ensured ritual purity. N. V. Joshi,
for example, reported numbers of new public eating houses run by
widows springing up in every quarter of Poona in his description of
the town in 1868, although, as he reported, 'if any timid gentlemen
eats in one of them, he is likely to come away hungry, because those
women never serve you enough to fill your stomach'.[200] Such
ventures attracted considerable hostility, as much, it seems for the
scandal of women living and earning independently as for suggestions of sexual impropriety, although for critics such as Joglekar at
least, the two amounted to exactly the same thing. Writing, he said,
'solely and deliberately to improve the state of high-caste people',
this lurid play depicted the widow Ganga as one of a number of
foul-mouthed and greedy proprietresses who made a fat living by
selling the sexual services of their suffering virgin daughters.[201]

Another widow, Mathurabai, runs a 'widows' club' at her house, where we see one of its members sitting in an easy chair reading a book, a sure sign of female dissoluteness.[202] For the sake of the whole community, Joglekar demanded, 'we must put a stop to these independent widows, and particularly those that run businesses selling food'.[203] When Tarabai referred, therefore, to widows and women who were no longer prepared to keep quiet because they could see that men were not keeping to the old religious values any more, she evidently spoke with good authority.[204]

CONCLUSIONS

Despite her relative youth when a *A Comparison between Women and Men* appeared in 1882, as well as her own evident powers of rhetoric and invective, Tarabai never published again. In this she was unlike the great majority of her male contemporaries, for whom authorship and publication usually represented ongoing activities engaged in over a number of years. Part of the reason for this may have been that her book was received with contempt and ridicule in one of the major Maratha newspapers of the time. This was the *Shetkarayanca Kaivari*, edited by Krishnarao Bhalekar, himself the author of numerous anti-brahmanical tracts. The original of this newspaper has not survived, but Jotirao Phule made a short reference to it in 1882, which suggests also that some at least of Tarabai's criticism may have been directed at men within her own Maratha circles. It was certainly true, Phule said, that her opinions had been very hotly stated.

> But one stupid newspaper editor at least did not like what she wrote, probably because he feared that the burden of all her accusations would fall around his own neck. So in order to denigrate Tarabai's book, he poured scorn on all the advice given in it and threw it down amongst the rubbish, and thus with great disdain repaid Tarabai's efforts by abusing her instead.[205]

This kind of public hostility may in part explain Tarabai's reticence in later life, for we hear nothing more of her, either directly or from

her male contemporaries, until S. G. Malshe's enquires in the early
1970s referred to above. In part, this may have been because she
was not working in the kind of liberal reformist milieu which,
elsewere in India, gave women writers like herself greater public
support and recognition although if she had been, her views might
well have been less forcible and interesting.[206]

Yet it is important that we rediscover the writing and lives of
such women, not only for what they can tell us about women, but
for their value in generating new questions and insights for a wider
social history. For, as I have argued, questions of gender had a
peculiar significance for politics and society for India in the
nineteenth century. First, and in particular for the old warrior-
peasant communities that have now come to constitute many of
India's 'dominant peasant' classes, the colonial peace meant a
search for new means both of expressing social distinction, and of
limiting and controlling social relations between strata of society
that had hitherto remained relatively flexible. For both of these
purposes, women and the development of more restrictive models
for their social behaviour assumed a considerable new importance.
Second, the politics of gender enabled colonial officials and key
groups of elite Indian men to find important areas of agreement.
Shifting as these may have been, it was from such links and
grounds for co-operation that the larger structures of colonial
hegemony were built.

If gender thus shaped key political relations in this period, it
was in turn shaped by them. Uma Chakravarty has argued that the
kind of womanhood invented in the nineteenth century has continued to be extremely influential in the twentieth, helping to
construct the 'Sati-Sita-Savitri' model that pervades much social
practice in the present day.[207] That womanhood, as we have seen it
constructed here, was a kind of Victorianized *pativrata*, with the
implication always of a peculiarly feminine moral vulnerability
underlying it. These models for womanhood, reinforced with
Hinduized forms of veiling and outward modesty for women, were
particularly important for emerging dominant peasant castes like
the Marathas, Jats and Rajputs in the later nineteenth century. As
Madhu Kishwar has noted, these newly hegemonic upper and
middle caste peasant groups now generate some of contemporary
India's most repressive cultures for women, and it is from them
that such models of female respectability are now being more

widely disseminated.[208] As was the case in the later nineteenth
century, moreover, many of these images and models continue to
be disseminated through forms of popular entertainment. With
their themes of submissive virgins, chastity under seige and
independent female sexuality punished, the nineteenth-century
writers discussed above would have been entirely at home with
much popular Indian cinema in the present day.[209]

In other ways, too, this was a crucial period for gender relations
in the wider context of politics, law and the state. As it was in
western societies, this was the period in India when large areas of
life affecting women were declared more firmly to be either
'domestic matters' beyond the state's competence, or, in the Indian
context, a matter of community 'religous' law, which the state was
competent only to administer. In the years after Tarabai wrote, of
course, these distinctions were replicated in the structure and
purely 'political' orientation of the Indian National Congress itself,
and marked out more clearly in the widening divide with the
National Social Conference. It was on the basis of these separate
domains, moreover, that so many writers and publicists of the
1880s and 1890s moved to develop contemporary images of
objectified femininity for more overt nationalist and religious
revivalist purposes, from Vivekananda's ideals of Aryan womanhood to Bankim Chandra Chatterjee's images of a sacred mother-
land.[210] It is in this context, as Uma Chakravarti has remarked, that
we can best explain the disappearance from the 1890s of women's
issues from the agenda of nationalist politics: they were no longer
compatible with these more deified forms of Hindu tradition and
Hindu womanhood.[211] Moreover, when women did begin to enter
the political arena as comrades in nationalist politics in the 1920s,
their roles continued to be shaped by many of the same themes,
and Indian 'tradition' itself constructed in the thinking of Gandhi
and others in the same images of idealized nineteenth century
femininity.[212]

These emerging trends were very much the focus of Tarabai's
concern. In some respects, her ideas remained limited and con-
strained by her own Maratha milieu and class. From these derived
the elements of nostalgia in her writing, although this nostalgia was
not without a certain logic of its own. While deriding all contemporary notions of *pativrata*, moreover, she did not entirely relin-
quish the idea itself. In other ways too, her writing emerges from an

oral culture in which women were dignified by their maternal and sexual power and by their capacity for personal devotion, although, as we have seen, these assertions of women's honour were easily turned into means of shaming and ridiculing men. Yet if the countermodels she offered were in many ways flawed and contradictory, her critique, and her sense of what these trends in contemporary politics and culture would mean for the future of women in 'modernizing' India, were no less pointed and effective.

Notes

1. Details of this case and of the Appeal Court hearing in Bombay are in the *Indian Spectator*, 27 May 1881.
2. Tarabai Shinde, *A Comparison between Women and Men*, Poona 1882. I refer to this henceforward as *A Comparison*.
3. A good example of this liberal approach is Stanley A. Wolpert, *Tilak and Gokhale: Revolution and Reform in the Making of Modern India*, University of California Press, Berkeley, 1961.
4. Lata Mani, 'Contentious Traditions: The Debate on *Sati* in Colonial India' in Kum Kum Sangari and Sudesh Vaid (eds.), *Recasting Women: Essays in Colonial History*, Kali for Women, New Delhi, 1989.
5. See, for example, Meredith Borthwick, *The Changing Role of Women in Bengal 1849–1905*, Princeton University Press, 1984, which also contains information about the first generation of Bengali women writers from the 1860s. These themes also run through the essays in Sangari and Vaid, *Recasting Women*; see also Madhu Kishwar, 'The daughters of Aryavarta' in J. Krishnamurty (ed.), *Women in Colonial India: Survival, Work and the State*, OUP, Delhi, 1989.
6. Borthwick, *The Changing Role of Women*, pp. 55–6.
7. See, for example, Susan Bayly, *Saints, Goddesses and Kings: Muslims and Christians in South Indian Society 1700–1900*, Cambridge University Press, 1990, especially the conclusion.
8. R. O'Hanlon, 'Gender, Discourse and Resistance in Colonial Western India' in D. Haynes and G. Prakash (eds.) *Contesting Power: Resistance and Everyday Social Relations in South Asia*, OUP, Delhi, 1991. This essay contains some of the arguments that I have put forward here.
9. See, for example, Partha Chatterjee, 'The Nationalist Resolution of the Woman's Question' in Sangari and Vaid, *Recasting Women*, p. 249.
10. Ibid., pp. 249–50.
11. For present-day oral accounts see, for example, K. Lalita et al, (eds.) '*We were Making History': Life Stories of Women in the Telengana People's Struggle*, Zed Books, London 1989, and Madhu Kishwar and Ruth Vanita, (eds.) *In Search of Answers: Indian Women's Voices from Manushi*, Zed Books, London 1984. More historical material will be in K. Lalita et al (eds.), *An Anthology of Women's Writings, 1830–1897*, Kali for Women, 1992.
12. See C. A. Bayly, *Rulers, Townsmen and Bazaars: North Indian Society in the Age of British Expansion, 1770–1870*, Cambridge University Press, 1983, pp. 48–51.
13. There is a large literature on these developments in Maratha history, but see in particular S. Chandra, 'Social background to the rise of the Maratha movement during the 17th century in India' in *Indian Economic and Social History Review*, September 1983; F. Perlin, 'Of White Whale and Countrymen in the Eighteenth Century Maratha Deccan: Extended Class Relations, Rights and the Problem of Rural Autonomy under the Old Regime' in the *Journal of Peasant Studies*, 5, 2 (1978); Andre Wink, *Land and Sovereignty in India: Agrarian Society and Politics under the Eighteenth Century Maratha Svarajya*, Cambridge University

Press, 1986; for the nineteenth century, R. O'Hanlon, *Caste, Conflict and Ideology: Mahatma Jotirao Phule and low caste protest in nineteenth century western India*, Cambridge University Press, 1985.

14. I have taken these details from S. G. Malshe's edited reprint of *A Comparison between Women and Men* published in 1975: S. G. Malshe, *Kai Tarabai Shindekrt Stri-purusha-tulana*, Mumbai Marathi Granthasangrahalaya, Bombay 1975, pp. 1–3.

15. See O'Hanlon, *Caste, Conflict and Ideology*, pp. 220–51.

16. *Marathmola* was defined in the mid-nineteenth century as 'ways and practices peculiar to the genuine Maratha', meaning in particular 'the non-appearance of the women of the house before strangers': J. T. Molesworth, *A Dictionary, Marathi and English*, Bombay 1957, p. 634.

17. For a general survey here, see Gunther Sontheimer, *The Hindu Joint Family*, New Delhi, 1977.

18. See, for example, Ramabai Ranade's account of opposition from senior women in the family when she was trying to learn to read in the 1870s: Ramabai Ranade, *Amchya ayushyatil kahi athvani*, Bombay 1910, pp. 57–8.

19. Quoted in Malshe, *Tarabai Shinde*, pp. 2–4.

20. Ibid., p. 3.

21. *A Comparison*, p. 77.

22. See below, pp. 48–50.

23. References to these western Indian examples are in R. D. Ranade, *Mysticism in Maharashtra*, Delhi, 1982. For Bahinabai in particular, see F. Hardy, 'The Diary of an Unknown Indian Girl', *Religion 1980*, and Anne Feldhaus, 'Bahina Bai: Wife and Saint', *Journal of the American Academy of Religion*, 1982, which has a good bibliography for women in *bhakti* more widely. Present-day examples are in Leela Mullatti, *The Bhakti Movement and the Status of Women*, New Delhi, 1989.

24. *A Comparison*, p. 75.

25. A discussion of this process is in Sangari and Vaid, *Recasting Women*, pp. 10–14 and for women and the state more generally, in Henrietta More, *Feminism and Anthropology*, Polity Press, Oxford, 1988, pp. 21–4.

26. Bayly, *Rulers, Townsmen and Bazaars*, pp. 11–12; David Washbrook and Burton Stein, 'States and societies: configuring state and capitalism in early modern India': mimeo, 1991.

27. Susan Bayly, *Saints, Goddesses and Kings*, especially pp. 453–9.

28. C. A. Bayly, *Indian Society and the Making of the British Empire*, Cambridge University Press, 1988, pp. 155–8.

29. For the importance of the Company's concern with texts here, see Nicholas B. Dirks, 'The invention of caste: civil society in colonial India', *Social Analysis*, no. 25, September 1989.

30. A recent introduction to these developments is in Kenneth W. Jones, *Socio-Religious Reform Movements in British India*, Cambridge University Press, 1989.

31. For these groups and processes, see Bayly, *Rulers, Townsmen and Bazaars*, pp. 208–9; J. Breman, *Of Peasants, Migrants and Paupers: Rural Labour Circulation and Capitalist Production in West India*, OUP, Delhi, 1985; Alice Clark, 'Limitations of female life chances in rural central Gujarat' in Krishnamurty (ed.), *Women in Colonial India*, and O'Hanlon, *Caste, Conflict and Ideology*, pp. 15–49.

32. Examples of such state intervention in Maratha domains are in H. Fukazawa, 'State and caste system (jati) in the eighteenth century Maratha kingdom', *Hitotsubashi Journal of Economics*, vol. 9, no. 1, June 1968.

33. See L. Carroll, 'Colonial Perceptions of Indian Society and the Emergence of Caste(s) Associations', *Journal of Asian Studies*, XXXVII, 2, 1978.

34. Clark, 'Limitations on female life chances', p. 41.

35 Chatterjee, 'The Nationalist Resolution', p. 249.

36. Mani, 'Contentious Traditions', p. 118.

37. Accounts of these are in Wamanrao M. Kolhatkar, 'Widow Remarriage' in C. Y. Chintamani (ed.), *Indian Social Reform*, Madras 1901, and Richard P. Tucker, 'From Dharmashastra to Politics', *Indian Economic and Social History Review*, 1970.

38. For these themes in brahmanic Hinduism see Susan Wadley, 'Women and the Hindu Tradition' in R. Ghadially (ed.), *Women in Indian Society*, New Delhi, 1988, and Julia Leslie, *The Perfect Wife: The Orthodox Hindu Woman according to the Stridharmapaddhati of Tryambakayajvan*, OUP, Delhi 1989.

39. Molesworth, *A Dictionary*, p. 690. See also Pandita Ramabai, *The High Caste Hindu Woman*, Maharashtra State Board for Literature and Culture Reprint, Bombay 1982, pp. 42–3.

40. Asok Sen, *Iswar Chandra Vidyasagar and his elusive milestones*, Riddhi-India, Calcutta, 1977.

41. Jones, *Socio-Religious Reform Movements*, pp. 141–4.

42. Tucker, 'From Dharmashastra to Politics', pp. 333–8.

43. Borthwick, 'The Changing Role of Women', pp. 55–9.

44. For this milieu, see I.M.P. Raeside, *Agarkar, Apte and the Kanitkars*, mimeo, n.d.

45. Some of these are described in Vir Talwar, 'Feminist Consciousness in Women's Journals in Hindi' in Sangari and Vaid, *Recasting Women*.

46. *Grihini*, August 1877. Walvekar was said to have started this extremely conventional and anodyne journal at the suggestion of Phule's wife Savitribai, who also contributed to it anonymously: G. G. Kale to P. S. Patil, Hadapsar, 21 November 1940, P. S. Patil MSS, reprinted in S. Raykar (ed.), *Amhi Pahilele Phule*, Poona 1981, pp. 20–1.

47. Raeside, 'Agarkar, Apte and the Kanitkars', p. 5.

48. Gordon Johnson, *Provincial Politics and Indian Nationalism: Bombay and the Indian National Congress 1880–1915*, Cambridge University Press, 1973, pp. 53–117.

49. The replies to this survey were published: *Selections from the Records of the Government of India in the Home Department, No. CCXXIII: Papers relating to Infant Marriage and Enforced Widowhood*, Government Printing Press, Calcutta 1886.

50. Wolpert, *Tilak and Gokhale*, pp. 35–7.

51. Ibid., pp. 37–8. This case is also described in Pandita Ramabai, *The High Caste Hindu Woman*, pp. 34–5.

52. See Padmini Sengupta, *Pandita Ramabai Saraswati: Her Life and Work*, Asia Publishing House, Bombay 1970; Uma Chakravarti, 'Whatever happened to the Vedic Dasi?' in Sangari and Vaid, *Recasting Women*, pp. 65–76, and especially Ram Bapat, *Pandita Ramabai*, MS.

53. As, for example, in Pandita Ramabai, *The High Caste Hindu Woman*, p. 35, or in her speech to the Third Session of the National Social Conference of 29 December 1889, quoted in Sengupta, *Pandita Ramabai*, pp. 193–5.

54. Bapat, *Pandita Ramabai*, p. 110.

55. Wolpert, *Tilak and Gokhale*, pp. 71–6.

56. O'Hanlon, *Caste, Conflict and Ideology*, pp. 117–21.

57. See Phule's response to the Government of India's 1884 survey: *Papers relating to Infant Marriage and Enforced Widowhood*, pp. 45–7; Raykar, *Amhi pahilele Phule*, pp. 26–7.

58. Jotirao Phule, *Satsar*, in D. Keer and S. G. Malshe (eds.), *Mahtma Phule: Samagra Vadmaya*, Bombay 1969, p. 293.

59. Ibid., p. 297.

60. *A Comparison*, p. 77.

61. As reflected, for example, in the title of the collection of essays edited by B.R.Nanda: *Indian Women from Purdah to Modernity*, New Delhi 1975. I am greatly indebted to Chris Bayly for a discussion on the themes of this section.

62. H. Papanek, 'Purdah: Separate Worlds and Symbolic Shelter' in H. Papanek and G. Minault (eds.), *Separate Worlds: Studies of Purdah in South Asia*, Delhi 1982, pp. 18–19. See also the discussion in Patricia Jeffery, *Frogs in a Well: Indian Women in Purdah*, Zed Books, London 1979, pp. 2–6. The *burqa* is the long concealing over-garment, now worn almost exclusively by Muslim women, for wear outside the home.

63. *A Dictionary of the Maratha Language, Compiled by Jugunnauth Shastree Kramuvunt and others in the service of the Bombay Education Society*, Bombay, 1829.

64. 'Some Account of the Productions and Peculiarities of the Mahratta Country': Miscellaneous Tracts, *Asiatic Annual Register*, 1803, pp. 54–5.

65. William Henry Tone, 'Illustrations of some Institutions of the Mahratta People', *Asiatic Annual Register*, 1798–9, p. 126.

66. 'A Memoir of the Bounsla family of Mahrattas', *Asiatic Annual Register*, 1801, p. 22.

67. T.D. Broughton, *Letters from a Mahratta Camp during the year 1809*, London 1892, p. 116.

68. Idem.

69. Richard Jenkins, *Report on the Territories of the Rajah of Nagpore submitted to the Supreme Government of India*, Calcutta 1827, p. 56.

70. Mirza Abu Taleb Khan, 'Vindication of the Liberties of the Asiatic Women', Miscellaneous Tracts, *Asiatic Annual Register*, 1801, p. 103. The same point is made in Borthwick, *The Changing Role of Women*, p. 5.

71. Tukaram Tatya Padval, *Jatibheda Vivekasara*, Bombay 1861, p. 54.

72. *Dnyanodaya*, 1 May 1861.

73. *Gazetteer of the Bombay Presidency: Sholapur*, Bombay 1884, p. 88.

74. Ibid., *Satara*, 1885, p. 76.

75. Ibid., *Nasik*, 1883, p. 48.

76. Ibid., *Ahmadnagar*, 1884, p. 87.

77. Ibid., p. 88.

78. *Central Provinces District Gazetteer: Buldhana District*, Calcutta 1910, p. 140.

79. *Kesari*, 25 April 1882.

80. R.V. Russell and Rai Bahadur Hira Lal (eds.), *The Tribes and Castes of Central India*, Calcutta 1916, vol. iv, p. 205–6.

81. *Central Provinces District Gazetteers: Amraoti District*, Bombay 1911, pp. 154–9. A *deshmukh* was a pre-colonial district-level headship. The British commuted these offices to political pensions, but still conferred them as rewards for loyal service.

82. *Buldhana District Gazetteer*, p. 124. Similar movements were reported in Amraoti, Yeotmal and Akola districts.

83. Desmukh Nilkanthrao Bhausaheb Khalatkar, *Marathance rudhi ani sudharana*, Nagpur 1907, p. 35.

84. Ibid., p. 24–5.

85. Ibid., p. 26.

86. Ibid., pp. 25–6.

87. Ibid., p. 26; '+ + +' in Marathi prose usually indicates matters too unseemly to mention.

88. M.A. Sherring, *Hindu Tribes and Castes as Represented in Benaras*, London 1872, vol. ii, pp. 76–7.

89. David Pocock, 'Bases of Faction in Gujarat', *British Journal of Sociology*, December 1957.

90. *A Comparison*, pp. 87–8.

91. As in C.A. Bayly, 'From Ritual to Ceremony: Death Ritual in Hindu North India since 1600' in J. Whaley (ed.), *Mirrors of Mortality: Studies in the Social History of Death*. Europa, London 1981, p. 173.

92. *A Comparison*, p. 92.

93. Chakravarti, 'Whatever Happened to the Vedic Dasi', p. 93.

94. Leslie, *The Perfect Wife*, p. 31.

95. Ibid., p. 101.

96. Ibid., p. 23.

97. Ibid., p. 303.

98. Fukazawa, 'State and caste system', p. 42; V.S. Kadam, 'The institution of marriage and position of women in eighteenth century Maharashtra', *Indian Economic and Social History Review*, 25, 3, 1988, p. 349.

99. Ibid., pp. 350–58.

100. T. Coats, 'Account of the Present State of the Township of Lony', *Transactions of the Literary Society of Bombay*, vol. iii, 1823, p. 202.

101. G.G. Jambhekar (ed.) *Memoirs and Writings of Acharya Bal Shastri Jambhekar*, Bombay 1950, vol. ii, p. 131.

102. A. Steele, *The Law and Custom of Hindoo Castes within the Dekhun Provinces subject to the Presidency of Bombay*, London, 1868, pp. xvii, 26, 101.

103. See, for example, Lucy Carroll, 'Law, custom and statutory social reform: the Hindu Widows' Remarriage Act of 1856' in *Indian Economic and Social History Review*, 20, 4, 1983, p. 364.

104. *A Comparison*, p. 75.

105. *Vichardarpan*, June 1860, no. 6, p. 48.

106. Tukaram Tatya Padval, *Jatibheda vivekasara*, Bombay 1865, p. 45.

107. Ibid., p. 52.

108. Ibid., p. 56.

109. Vithoba Sonaji Chavan, *Bhandari Lokanca Vrattant*, Bombay 1887, pp. 62–3. I am indebted to Pratibha Ranade for this reference.

110. *Dnyanodaya*, 15 September 1865.

111. *Papers relating to Infant Marriage and Enforced Widowhood*, p. 195.

112. Ibid., p. 97.

113. Ibid., p. 101.

114. Ibid., p. 108.

115.   N.M Lokhande, *Panch Darpan: useful regulations of all the castes*, Bombay 1876, p. 25.

116.   Phule, *Samagra Vadmaya*, p. 361.

117.   *Imperial Census of 1881: Operations and Results in the Presidency of Bombay*, Central Government Press, Bombay, 1882, vol. ii, pp. xli–xlvii.

118.   Ibid., vol. i, pp. 83, 85, 89.

119.   Carroll, 'Law, custom and statutary social reform', p. 379.

120.   James Forbes, *Oriental Memoirs*, London 1813, vol. i, p. 210; V.L. Birze, *Kshatriya va tyance astitva*, Baroda 1903, p. 345.

121.   Prem Chowdhry, 'Customs in a Peasant Economy: Women in Colonial Haryana' in Sangari and Vaid, *Recasting Women*; David Pocock, *Kanbi and Patidar: A study of the Patidar Community of Gujarat*, Clarendon, Oxford, 1972, p. 64.

122.   *A Comparison*, p. 77.

123.   *Shivaji*, 1 July 1881, *Report on Native Newspapers for the Bombay Presidency*, week ending 9 July 1881.

124.   *A Comparison*, p. 93.

125.   *Subodha Patrika*, 29 May 1881; ibid., week ending 4 June 1881.

126.   *Bombay Samachar*, 15 June 1881; ibid., week ending 18 June 1881.

127.   *Times of India*, 17 May 1881.

128.   *Indian Spectator*, 27 May 1881.

129.   *A Comparison*, p. 117.

130.   There is a growing literature here, but see for example Sumanta Banerjee, 'Marginalization of Women's Popular Culture in Nineteenth Century Bengal' in Sangari and Vaid, *Recasting Women*, and Ashis Nandy, *The Intimate Enemy: Loss and Recovery of Self under Colonialism*, OUP, Delhi, 1983.

131.   I.M.P. Raeside, 'Early Prose Fiction in Marathi' in T.W. Clark (ed.), *The Novel in India: Its Birth and Development*, London, 1970.

132.   *Dnyanodaya* 15 July 1864.

133.   When Pandita Ramabai needed to raise money for her visit to England in 1882, she also wrote a book on *pativrata* and morals for women: Sengupta, *Pandita Ramabai*, p. 99. The book is a collection of 'improving' moral homilies, its subjects including 'Education', 'Behaving with restraint', 'Housekeeping' and 'Care and education of children'. Pandita Ramabai, *Stridharmaniti*, Poona 1882.

134.   Ramjee Gunnojee, *Stree Churitra or Female Narration*, Bombay 1882, p. 2.

135.   Ibid., p. 1.

136.   Ibid., p. 423.

137.   Ibid., p. 84.

138.   *A Comparison*, p. 114. Chintaman Dixit Joshi, *Vidagdha Stri Charita*, Satara 1871.

139.   Govind Vinayak Kanitkar, *Sushikshita Stricharitra*, Bombay 1872, introduction.

140.   Ibid., p. 67.

141.   Ibid., p. 115.

142.   Ibid., p. 67.

143.   *A Comparison*, p. 113.

144.   Ibid., p. 100.

145.   Naro Sadashiv Risbud, *Manjughosha*, Poona 1875, pp. 63–4.

146.   Shridhar was a sixteenth century brahman poet of Pandharpur in western India, who wrote extremely popular Marathi versions of the *Ramayana* and *Mahabharata*.

147.   *A Comparison*, p. 115.

148. Ibid., p. 119.
149. Mahadev Balkrishna Chitale, *Manorama Nataka*, Bombay 1871, p. vii.
150. Ibid., pp. 140–1.
151. Ibid., pp. 167–76.
152. Ibid., pp. 195–6.
153. *A Comparison*, p. 117.
154. Ibid., p. 107.
155. Ibid., pp. 92, 110–1.
156. Ibid., p. 113.
157. *Dnyanodaya*, 1 May 1865.
158. Ibid., 1 September 1865.
159. Kashinath Balkrishna Marathe, *Naval va natak yavishayi nibandha*, Bombay 1872, pp. 5–7.
160. Ibid., p. 35.
161. Laxman Moreshvar Halbe, *Muktamala*, Bombay 1851, introduction.
162. D.V. Tahmankar, *Lokamanya Tilak*, London 1956, p. 41.
163. *A Comparison*, p. 119.
164. Ibid., p. 93.
165. Ibid., p. 99.
166. Ibid., p. 76.
167. See discussion above, pp. 4–5.
168. Tone, 'Illustrations', p. 144; Broughton, 'Letters', p. 94.
169. Bayly, *Rulers, Townsmen and Bazaars*, p. 116. For women's access to power see in particular Stuart Gordon, 'Legitimacy and Loyalty in some Successor States of the Eighteenth Century' in J.F. Richards (ed.), *Kingship and Authority in South Asia*, University of Wisconsin-Madison, 1981.
170. For Maratha examples, see B.G. Gokhale, *Poona in the Eighteenth Century: An Urban History*, OUP, Delhi 1988, pp. 48, 107–137. Gopikabai, for example, was the very influential wife of the peshwa Balaji Bajirao, and linked his government with her own powerful Raste family of bankers.
171. Wink, *Land and Sovereignty*, pp. 101–2; G.S. Sardesai, *New History of the Marathas*, vol. iii, Bombay, 1968, pp. 211–5; John Malcolm, A *Memoir of Central India*, New Delhi, 1970, vol. i, p. 316. Malcolm praised Tulsabai's horsemanship, 'an essential quality in a Mahratta lady'.
172. Sardesai, *New History of the Marathas*, p. 338.
173. Ibid., p. 18; Gokhale, *Poona in the Eighteenth Century*, pp. 118–9; 'A Memoir of the Bounsla family of Mahrattas', p. 22; M.G. Ranade, *Rise of the Maratha Power*, Bombay 1900, pp. 134–5; Malcolm, *Central India*, vol. i, p. 103.
174. James Forbes, *Oriental Memoirs*, vol. iii, p. 323; Wink, *Land and Sovereignty*, p. 107; Leslie, *The Perfect Wife*, p. 20.
175. Ibid., pp. 21–2; Gokhale, *Poona in the Eighteenth Century*, pp. 72–3; S.V. Desai, *Social Life in Maharashtra under the Peshwas*, Bombay 1980, p. 74.
176. See, for example, the Rani of Jhansi's strategies here, described in W.H. Sleeman, *Rambles and Recollections of an Indian Official*, London 1893, vol. i. p. 256.
177. Ibid., p. 310.
178. For the transition in western India, see R.D. Choksey, *Mountstuart Elphinstone: The Indian Years*, Bombay 1971.

179. See for example Sleeman, *Rambles and Recollections*, vol i, p. 256, for the Rani of Jhansi and J.S.Lushington, 'On the Marriage Rites and Usages of the Jats of Bharatpur', *Journal of the Asiatic Society*, no. 18, June 1833, pp. 274–5, for the Regent of Bharatpur.

180. Sleeman, *Rambles and Recollections*, vol. i. p. 310.

181. O'Hanlon, 'Gender, Discourse and Resistance', pp. 76–9.

182. Chatterjee, 'The Nationalist Resolution', p. 249.

183. *Papers Relating to Infant Marriage and Enforced Widowhood*, p. 187.

184. *A Comparison*, p. 93–4.

185. Ibid., p. 85.

186. Ibid., p. 96.

187. Ibid., p. 122.

188. idem.

189. Ibid., p. 124. For a twentieth-century example of this kind of ethic, see D. Jacobson, 'The chaste wife: cultural norm and individual experience' in S. Vatuk (ed.), *American Studies in the Anthropology of India*, Manohar, New Delhi 1978.

190. Wadley, 'Women and the Hindu Tradition'; David Kinsley, *Hindu Goddesses: Visions of the Divine Feminine in the Hindu Religious Tradition*, Delhi 1987; J. Hawley and D. Wulf (eds.), *The Divine Consort: Radha and the Goddesses of India*, University of California Press, Berkeley, 1982.

191. Bayly, *Saints, Goddesses and Kings*, p. 28ff.

192. References are given in the notes to Tarabai's text.

193. *Dnyanprakash*, 6 August 1855.

194. *Vichardarpan*, October 1860, no. 10, p. 76.

195. *Indu Prakash*, 29 January 1883.

196. *Papers Relating to Infant Marriage and Enforced Widowhood*, pp. 49–50.

197. Ibid., p. 171.

198. Director of Ethnography for India, MSS Eur. D. 356, Position of Widows, Oriental and India Office Collections. I am indebted to Vidyut Bhagwat for this reference. Another contemporary warning story was that the long hair of widows would bind their husbands in hell: Sengupta, *Pandita Ramabai*, p. 194.

199. D.V. Joglekar, *Independent Widows and their Youthful Daughters*, Bombay 1888. K.B. Marathe refers to *Svairasvakesha* as another example of literature preoccupied with immoral women: *Naval va natak*, p. 35.

200. N.V. Joshi, *Punevarnana*, Bombay 1868, p. 138. High-caste widows had often been able to get work as cooks: see the case cited in *Papers Relating to Infant Marriage and Enforced Widowhood*, p. 47.

201. Joglekar, *Independent Widows*, p. 1.

202. Ibid., p. 24.

203. Ibid., p. 34.

204. *A Comparison*, p. 94.

205. Phule, Satsar, p. 297.

206. E. Fox-Genovese, 'Culture and Consciousness in the Intellectual History of European Women', *Signs*, vol. 12, no. 3, 1987.

207. Chakravarti, 'Whatever happened to the Vedic Dasi?', p. 79. These are, of course, the names of women from Hindu mythology connoting the virtues of the 'new' woman.

208. Madhu Kishwar, *In Search of Answers*, pp. 8–13.

209. See S. Dasgupta and R. Hegde, 'The Eternal Receptacle: A Study of Mistreatment of Women in Hindi Films' in R. Ghadially (ed.), *Women in Indian Society*, New Delhi, 1988.

210. Uma Chakravarti, 'Whatever happened to the Vedic *Dasi*? pp. 49–60.'

211. Ibid., p. 76.

212. Madhu Kishwar, 'Gandhi on Women', *Race and Class*, Summer 1986; Sujata Patel, 'The Construction and Reconstruction of Woman in Gandhi', Nehru Memorial Museum and Library: *Occasional Papers in History and Society*, no. 49.

स्त्रीपुरुषतुलना.

अथवा

स्त्रिया व पुरुष यांत साहसी कोण हैं स्पष्ट करून दाखविण्याकरितां हा निबंध

ताराबाई शिंदे यानीं रचिला.

बुलठाणें.

प्रांत व-हाड.

पुणें येथें
" श्री शिवाजी " छापखान्यांत छापिलें.
सन १८८२ इ०
किंमत ९ आणे.

A COMPARISON BETWEEN
WOMEN AND MEN

An essay to show who's really wicked and immoral,
women or men?

Tarabai Shinde

Buldhana

Varhad Province

Printed at 'Shri Shivaji' Press, Pune

1882

Price 9 annas

Introduction

God brought this amazing universe into being, and he it was also who created men and women both.[1] So is it true that only women's bodies are home to all kinds of wicked vices?[2] Or have men got just the same faults as we find in women? I wanted this to be shown absolutely clearly, and that's the reason I've written this small book, to defend the honour of all my sister countrywomen. I'm not looking at particular castes or families here. It's a comparison just between women and men.

Now, about the custom of widow remarriage. It's just not true these days that only the brahman castes stop their widows getting married again. Lots of other castes and families do the same: Prabhus, Shenvis, Gujaratis, Bhatias, Marwadis, Marathas, Desais, Deshmukhs, Inamdars; and Marathas with names like Shirke, Mahadik, Jadhav, Bhosle and Mane, families from places like Sholapur, Satara, Pune, Gwalior and Indore, the very families who died for the Maratha power.[3] You can see an even stricter rule than the brahmans in their families against the remarriage of widows. In these people's houses you can wait till the end of your life, and it won't happen. If one husband goes off and dies, too bad—they'll never let you have another one.

The second thing I want to write about is that it's not just one part of the country that's taken on English people's habits, or one caste. Take the way people dress. The customs of all castes have changed, even of our kings and princes. What's happened now to all those places that once made silk brocade, costumes of silver and gold, aigrettes of jewels for turbans, turbans embroidered with gold, lengths of cloth from Chanderi, nine-yard saris from Paithan, gold-bordered headdresses, woven dhotis from Nagpur, soft red leather slippers ?[4] When women's husbands take up new manners and habits, women start trying to do just the same themselves. They haven't got the fashion yet of wearing full-length gowns, like English women. But they've already started puting on coats, jackets with fancy pleats and long sleeves and shoes and stockings on their feet.

These days, women only want to wear one mangalsutra round their necks, with just one string of delicate little beads, and it's the same with the kumkum they have to put on their foreheads, out of shame for what people will think if they don't. They put it between their brows, a little dot smaller than a split pea, leaving all of the rest of their foreheads completely white and bare![5] Nowadays women also feel shy about their jewellery, just as men feel ashamed to wear all the old kinds of neck ornaments and rings. They prefer to go round looking as plain as Parvati in white or coloured cloth costing just a couple of rupees, with a pure white blouse of muslin or chintz.[6] So the main point I want to make here is that the fine circumstances we used to have in our country are all gone now, all turned to bad. Those beautiful saris from Paithan which used to sell at five hundred rupees each, they've all gone now. Towns like Dhanavad, Nagpur, Barhanpur, Sholapur, Ahmedabad, have all hidden their faces.[7] Instead of theirs every house now flies a different sort of flag, in long lengths of fine foreign cloth.

In fact, it's you men and these worthless fads and fancies of yours that have wrecked all our own native ways of making a living, so our tradesmen and skilled craft people are all perishing of hunger. Our glory has all been driven away and Lakshmi, who all of you press to make her home in yours, she's seen these fads, these dirty defiling habits of yours and she's taken herself away now, on the road to a distant country.[8] So I place this little book before you, so you might have some pity for women who are widows, and for the wives and children of these poor working folk. I'm doing it to make you men open your eyes and take a new look at your country and have some pride in it, rather than each one of you just abandoning the dharma, habits and customs of his own country. I'm doing it out of the hope that you might stop treating all women as though they had committed a crime and making their lives a hell for it.

Of course, I'm just a poor woman without any real intelligence, who's been kept locked up and confined in the proper old Maratha manner.' This is my very first effort, so the book has passages that are disconnected and fragmentary, and it's written in the rough and harsh language of the Marathas of old. But every day now we have to look at some new and more horrible example of men who are really wicked and their shameless lying tricks. And not a single person says anything about it. Instead people go about pinning the blame on women all the time, as if everything bad was their fault! When I saw this, my whole mind just began churning and shaking out of feeling for the honour of womankind. So I lost all my fear, I just couldn't stop myself writing about it in this very biting language. In fact, if I could have found even stronger words to describe how you men all stick together and cover up for each other, I would have used them in my clumsy way. Because you men are all the same, all full of lies and dirty tricks. But I come from the weaker side of nature, so you'll see all sorts of faults in this book. With powerful intellects like yours you'll find all types of criticisms to level at it, and all sorts of ways to sing the praises of your own kind instead. Still, all I've done here is write down what I see with my eyes. I'm not going to ask all the usual things here—don't just ignore this book, read it carefully, give it some support and so on. All I ask is if you're really someone with an open mind, think about it carefully and see if what I say is true or not. But if you just kick your horses forward to protect those fancy reputations of yours, I've got no remedy for that. Still, I will myself always struggle and strive for the good of my own kind, and keep on sowing the seed of good conduct in their minds.

Tarabai Shinde

p.78 bla.

A Comparison between Women and Men

These days the newspapers are always writing about poor helpless women and the wicked things they do. Why won't any of you come forward and put a stop to these great calamities?

Just look now, how the custom of not remarrying widows has spread—in so many places, to so many castes, like a great sickness. It's hard to imagine the bitter despair all these hundreds and thousands of widows must suffer. And how many disasters come out of it. Because stridharma hasn't ever been saved just by making people sit at home and control their thoughts.[10] What they do with their minds and eyes can make them just as guilty. Where does it get you if you snatch away all the happy signs of a woman's marriage, if you chop off one woman's hair and wipe off another's kumkum from her forehead? Women still have the same hearts inside, the same thoughts of good and evil. You can strip the outside till it's naked, but you can't do the same to the inside, can you? In fact, what does stridharma really mean? It means always obeying orders from your husband and doing everything he wants. He can kick you and swear at you, keep his whores, get drunk, gamble with dice and bawl he's lost all his money, steal, commit murder, be treacherous, slander people, rob peoples' treasures or squeeze them for bribes. He can do all this, but when he comes home, stridharma means women are meant to think, 'Oh, Who's this coming now but our little lord Krishna, who's just stolen the milkmaids' curds and milk and tried to blame Chandravali for it'.[11]

And then smile at him and offer their devotion, stand ready at his service as if he was Paramatma himself. But how can people go on believing this idea of stridharma once they've begun to think about what's good and bad? They'd change their ideas straightaway, wouldn't they? A man can run off with someone else's wife, but that's not against the rule of pativrata.[12] In fact, there are thousands of reasons for breaking the rule. You're supposed to worship your husband as if he were a god. But who is there nowadays that really does? There's that story of Savitri[13], which sets out an example of pativrata. Would any woman now try to follow it all to the letter? Go on then, can you show us even one?

That story tells us that if a husband kicks you, you should just smile at him and say, 'Don't do that, my lord and husband: you'll hurt your foot'. And so saying, you should sit down and promptly start massaging his foot. You're not to cry if he lets you have it with his fist, even if he beats you with a stick. No, you've got to smile, fetch fresh butter and rub it into his hands for him, saying, 'My lord, the palm of your hand must be burning from those blows'. And if there's no butter in the house, use the neighbour's, and if she's got none, run and get some from the market. But who'd do any of this nowadays? Far from stroking his hand, she'd more likely tell him to shove it in the stove. If he dislikes a particular sort of food, she's meant to avoid it too. It's just the opposite though— he throws it down and she picks it up straight. It's got to be something sweet though! If it's some ordinary old vegetable like carrots or gourd, then fine, she'll avoid them for life! But if it's mangoes the husband won't eat, will she give them up? Not a bit![14] If the husband asks for water, she's not standing ready with a clean brass vessel. Instead the lady will tell him, 'Oh yes, I'm dying for some water, there's some in that pot over there, get yourself some, and get me some while you're at it! What am I supposed to do? This child here just won't let me get up'.

The husband's only got to mention his bath and she's meant to lay out the stool, get a bucket of hot water and stand ready to scrub his feet. But actually she just calls out, 'Anyone out here? Come in here, Ramya boy, he wants to have a bath, fetch him water and fold his dhoti for him. If he asks for me, tell him I'm having my tea'. As soon as her husband comes in for dinner, she's meant to bring a stool, lay out vessels for drinking, serve him his favourite foods, then sit wasting her time entertaining him with talk till he's finished his feast. But nowadays he'll be saying, 'Have you finished in there or not? Come on, serve it up, it's nine o'clock!' And the answer comes from her: 'All right, I'm coming, it's nearly ready. Can't you even wait till the vegetables and lentils are done? What, do you want me to serve you uncooked rice? What a chore this business is, every bloody day at nine o'clock! Every day the same hurry!' Then comes the subject of his roll of betel nut, and off they go again.[15] He calls out, 'Make me some betel, will you? The dish is in that niche in the wall over there. No, no, not like that—can't you even roll betel nut properly? You take all the ingredients together in your hand, like this'. So the lord and master goes over to the dish and looks inside, only to find there's no lime. 'Look, there's no lime', he says. 'Go and get some, will you?' But all he gets out of her is, 'There's some supari nut in a little bag in that box up there. You eat your betel and get one of those out for me. Ugh—doesn't your mouth feel nasty when you finish eating?' Well now—isn't this much closer to the truth?

This is what pativrata means these days. If I was to tell you the whole of it from start to finish, it'd take a whole separate book. Who on earth really follows the shastras to the letter or expects anyone else to?[16] If the husband is really to be like a god to the wife then shouldn't he behave like one? And if wives are to worship them like true devotees, shouldn't husbands have a tender love for them in return, and care about their joys and pains like a real god would? When the gods see those who worship them, they feel happy and satisfied. Shouldn't husbands be the same? When husbands find virtues or faults in people devoted to them, shouldn't they take a proper account of them, accept their shortcomings and correct them with love? What woman could really treat her husband like a god, no matter how nasty he was? The Pandavas' uncle Dhritarashtra was blind, so his wife Gandhari tied a cloth over her eyes when they were married.[17] But what person with eyes could stand to be told to close them and carry on as if they were blind? Who'd have the self-control for that? I don't know anyone. All your big talk—you make it all up on the basis of the shastras. But in fact the people who wrote all these books ought to be ashamed of themselves, shastras, puranas, pothis and so on.[18] You ask me why? Well, when they picked out women from previous ages, some of them had gone wrong too, but there they are now, held up as first-class pativratas. That's good, is it? Take Draupadi—she was a woman who had five husbands already, but that never stopped her from lusting secretly after Maharaja Karna, did it?[19] Ahalya sat in Surendra's lap, got turned to stone, then she became divine.[20] Satyavati and Kunti were supposed to be virgins, but they each had a son Vyas, the author of the Vedas, and Karna himself—but their names are still on the list. One of them believed what the sage told her because he got rid of the nasty smell on her body. The other just wanted to try out the magic mantra![21] Aren't all these gods and sages of yours wonderful? Each one better than the last! Each of them made a secret love marriage[22], then went off and got hitched to Shantanu and Panduraja! So what else were they doing but marrying a second time? Then their kids Vyas and big-hearted Karna got so holy even the gods fell down at their feet. But when someone has kids like that these days they get called very different names. A female slave's child gets put into one class of bastard, a brahman widow's into another; then there are cases like Vidur.[23] Other people put kids like that down as just another source of expense. So tell me what we should call it when an unmarried girl has a child? Someone like Vyas gets to be a great expert in shastras and puranas and writes books like the Mahabharata. Does that make his mother and father all pure again too? I reckon Karna's mother only got her virtue back when he fought with the Pandavas on the battlefield of Kurukshetra.

Then there's the story of Tara, wife of Vali the monkey. Sugriva was Vali's younger brother, but Vali carried off his wife Ruma and drove Sugriva the black-faced monkey away, long tail and all. Then Sugriva met up with Maharaja Ramchandra himself. They found they were in the same boat. Ramchandra's wife was stolen by Ravana, and Sugriva's by his own brother. So what a good thing, they joined up together! Ramchandra felt sorry for Sugriva, so he killed Vali by a cunning trick and fixed it up for Sugriva to marry Tara. Poor Tara said to Ramchandra, 'Maharaj, how can you do this? Your husband's younger brother is like your own child. This looks all wrong to me'. So Ramchandra reassured her: 'Don't you worry about it. You can marry a second time, even your husband's younger brother, and your name will still be counted among pativratas'.[24] All this went on. Then Shridhar Swami wrote a couple of extra lines saying it doesn't matter what the gods have done.[25] Of course, it doesn't mean that human beings are allowed to as well. But did the Swami never realize everyone would copy these examples and make them into models to be strictly followed? What else would they do? As for the Swami, he got carried away describing the crowds at Sugriva's coronation, all the confusion and extravagances and so on. Otherwise, he'd have probably written even more verses to put the fear of God into people!

Now, when that lad Ravana carried off the lady Sita he soon found he'd made a mistake. He got really besotted with her, sighing and groaning and all the rest. But if today's laws had been operating, the whole matter would have been settled quite simply. Ravana just would have handed over a few hundred thousand rupees to Rama towards his marriage expenses! The poor thing would have been left to live out his days happily, and people would never say of him that he lost his kingdom for a woman. But what was he to do? The god Brahma put a curse on him: 'If you lay violent hands on someone else's wife, your body will shatter into a hundred pieces'. He was terrified by the curse, and because of that he decided to die on the battlefield.[26] Otherwise, he'd have had to fork out money enough for ten weddings, and do his best to make sure Sita never saw Ayodhya again. He tried everything in his power, but he was finished. But wait—here's another example of pativrata. What is it? Ravana went to his wife Mandodari, and told her, 'You're a great pativrata—go and persuade Sita, make her believe she's like a sister to you—like a joint wife'. In those days, wives treated the command of a husband with great reverence. If you were carrying out the command of your husband, there was nothing wrong even in lying to another man's wife and procuring her for your husband, if that was what he wanted. Mandodari thought this was pativrata pure and blameless. So she went to see the lady, full of wise advice. 'See, Rama and Ravana are under the same sign of the zodiac. The first letters of his name are Ra; and Ravana's are just the same. And just look at everything our great demon Ravana's got— his feats of courage, his wealth and luxury, his great kingdom. Anyway, what would there be for you back there in Ayodhya? Nothing but living in the jungle, no house, no kingdom, nothing but disgrace'.[27] She lavished all this advice on Sita, but the lady wouldn't have any of it. Because Sita knew all about a different side to the story, about when the peasant woman humiliated Ravana in Baliraja's house, tying him upside down to Angada's cradle so he had to drink the child's pee, and the poor old chap couldn't do anything about it. So Sita told Mandodari some blunt home truths in return and sent her away.[28] That was the story of that little episode. But as for Mandodari herself, there was nothing wrong at all in obeying her husband's command to deceive someone else's wife with her devotion as a pativrata and deliver her over to satisfy his pleasure. Just the opposite, the names of people like Mandodari are celebrated all through the puranas. So this is really a story with two morals. The husband's happy because his wife carried out her great duty of seeing to his pleasures, and the wife's happy because she thinks she's done the proper thing. But it's poor old number three who falls in the snare for it, the first two don't care a damn! Oh, congratulations, all you gods! And three cheers for pativrata!

In fact, shouldn't we think of putting some of the blame on the gods themselves for all this? After all, what's the real truth here? Let the real truth be as it may—what our shastras tell us is that we shouldn't hesitate to kill a father or a brother if we find them against us on the battlefield. Seeing Lakshman strike Indrajit down, Ramchandra cried out, 'Lakshman, my brother, what are you doing? Oh, this dharma of warriors is so hard and heavy. To have regard for no one, not for your son-in-law, not even your own son'. At that point, and seeing Śulochana's devotion as a pativrata, Rama should have raised up Indrajit again and brought him back to life. But Rama listened to Maruti and Bibhishan stirring things up, so he just left that rare jewel of a woman to be thrown in the fire and be burnt.[29] Anyway, I just have to point out things like these, when they're true and there right in front of me. I'll say my prayers to the gods and ask them to excuse me if I've thrown a bit of blame on two or three of them here. They may forgive me, they may not; they'll go on being gods in any case. What about the sages of those days? One of them was born of a deer: that's Shringarishi; one of a bird, and that was Bharadvaj; one of an ass, Gardha-bharishi; and one of a cow, Vrishabharishi.[30] So each of them ended up writing their names after the animals they were born out of. They're all gone now, but women are still stuck with living up to it all. And you, what remedy have you got for it?

Oh yes, you've got the courage of lions, you do labours as great as Bhagiratha, you're as wise as Jaimini; oh, you've become such brave and fearless heroes, defeating great unconquerable enemies and turning them loose as if they were mere goats.[31] You catch hold of a great fierce god of fire like Agni in your fist and make him work any way you want through machines for all types of purposes. Vayu the wind is even stronger than Agni; you can see Agni with your eyes, sometimes even hold him in your hand, but you can't hold Vayu in your hand, you can't even see him, but you men have used your power to bring even him under control. Lightning is the mother of all, she lives high up in the infinite sky, surrounded by clouds where even the birds don't go. Yet you've dragged even her down, and put her to toil for you like a female slave. Seeing as you're such almighty heroes, why is it so impossible for you to pull poor widows out of this pit of shame? Why can't you break some caste rules, put the kumkum back on their foreheads and let them enjoy the happiness of marriage again?

Oh, all your superiority and courage—it never gets outside the house! It's just like when there's a blind old mother sitting in the middle with five or six little boys playing round her, and one of them says, 'I wanna be king!', and the second one says, 'Mummy, I'm the minister', and the third says, 'I'm the general of the army! Now, let's make a kingdom! This is the army! This is the king's court!' This is how you go on, all just floods of water in a mirage. Not one of you has really dared pick up the hero's challenge.[32] You're all just like the mice in council in Aesop's fables: 'Oh, we must tie the bell around the cat's neck, mustn't we?' This is so true: your mouths are full of talk about reform, but who actually does anything? You hold these great meetings, you turn up at them in your fancy shawls and embroidered turbans, you go through a whole ton of supari nut, cartloads of betel leaves, you hand out all sorts of garlands, you use up a tank full of rosewater, then you come home. And that's it. That's all you do. These phoney reform societies of yours have been around for thirty, thirty-five years. What's the use of them? You're all there patting yourselves on the back, but if we look closely, they're about as much use as a spare tit on a goat.

See now—God, who decides everything in this world, has used his great intelligence to fill the world with all sorts of fascinating things. But two things drag people's minds towards them strongest of all: wealth, and women. Out of these, women are even more piercing than money. They fill your lives with pleasures a thousand times greater than any money could give you. Just imagine—you could build a wonderful palace and live in it surrounded by luxury, with the most beautiful gardens, with all sorts of costly and exotic possessions, carriages, horses, chariots, palanquins, elephants, camels, armies, with servant retinues who waited on your every word, with all the pomp of the court. Would you set all this up for yourself, and leave out women? If you did, it would seem more like a burning ground than a palace, your stately golden couch and its warm bed of pillows just like a funeral pyre, and all that company of armies, companions and servants not friends but enemies. All your rich delicacies would feel bitter as lemons in your mouth, your fine robes and jewelled ornaments like snakes winding round you. It would send you crazy, all of it. Even if God himself came and stood before you, you'd drive him off that very instant, no doubt about it. Think how you'd feel, then ask yourself again—how can a woman be happy without men? She'd be in just the same state as you. Put her in whatever wonderful luxury you like, give her the whole world, but if she's alone, you just see what condition she'd be in. It's God's own wish that the two should be joined as a pair. Can't you see, God has created female in everything he's made, from the birds on down even to inanimate trees and plants. There's no grace or beauty in anything without matching pairs. No work gets done that's not done in pairs. Can you make your way in this wilderness of a world all on your own? Can you manage all the business of worldly life yourself? Can you really draw the plough over that great field all on your own, or live like a sanyasi[33] even for a month or two without seeing a woman's face? Without a woman by your side, your own uncle, even your father would hesitate to stand you up alongside a couple. Who cares about a stray solitary man all on his own?

If a man with a wife and children gets into difficulties through his vices or his virtues, if he falls out of favour with someone or gets in trouble with moneylenders, people say, 'Oh, but have a thought for his poor children'. No one really cares about the man himself. People only let him off for the sake of his wife and children. Even Agastya refused to take his darshan of Ramchandra without Sita.[34] When Ravana carried her off, he carried off Rama's very own strength. All he could do was wander helplessly through the wilderness, crying piteously, 'Oh my love, oh daughter of Janaka, river of virtue, oh Sita, Sita'. This is the sort of victorious power women possess.[35] Now, you can attack a strong enemy with great armies, with powder and shot and all sorts of murderous weapons, and make your enemy just a slave in chains. Countless strong kings can fall around you and blood flow like a swollen river, so in the end victory smiles on you. You might be able to catch a tiger and throw it in a trap, even saddle up a fierce wild animal like a lion, put a bit in its mouth and ride it round like a horse. But all your bravery and your shining heroism shrivel up in front of this little slip of a woman and the piercing glance of her eyes, and you fall down licking her feet like a dog. Any fool can pick up a sword or some weapon and hurt someone, there's no great heroism in that. But it's something else to be able to look at someone from a distance and set them sighing, aah, aah, with just a glance.[36] Who's more powerful now then? That woman or you?

It's the same even with your mother. She loves you beyond what she cares for herself, she watches over your life in times of trouble even more than when you were a child. She flashes to your command quick as lightning, she takes care in all sorts of ways that no blows should land on your honour in this worldly life, and when you look up there she is at your service, a sweet saint who bears everything in times of sorrow or of joy, sweet to the end. The point is it's her, who's always trying to make you happy, that you're heaping all this blame on to—it's her you're trying to push down to the bottom of the earth.[37] Aren't you ashamed? Oh, you idiots, women are shy, delicate and foolish in their very natures. And you, what lords you are, naturally so bold, courageous, strong, learned—so there you are calling women all these names, even before your lips have touched the nectar from your mother's golden breast. But just because you happen to be strong, does that make it right? You label women with all sorts of insulting names, calling them utterly feeble, stupid, bold, thoughtless—you beat out the sound of their names in shame. You shut them up endlessly in the prison of the home, while you go about building up your own importance, becoming Mr, Sir and so on. So you think to yourselves: what's a wife matter, after all? 'The hunter's him who's got the rabbit in his hand', and everything else is just stupid nonsense.[38] Starting from your childhood you collect all rights in your own hands and womankind you just push in a dark corner far from the real world, shut up in purdah, frightened, sat on, dominated as if she was a female slave.[39] And all the while you go about dazzling us all with the light of your own virtue. Learning isn't for women, nor can they come and go as they please. Even if a woman is allowed to go outside, the women she meets are ignorant like her, they're all just the same. So how's she ever going to get any greater understanding or intelligence?

Can any of these ancestors of yours produce any evidence direct from God that it's best for a wife to die before her husband, or a husband before his wife? Who lives and who dies is all in the hands of the all-powerful Narayan. Next to him, what stones are in your hands to throw? Is there a law about young people dying or old people living? Isn't it true that some people die just as they're born, some in the full flush of youth, some not till they've lived to be a hundred and taken full experience of the world; that some die when they're at the very peak of happiness? Isn't it true that some kings abandon their thrones as soon as Yama's messenger calls them and leave it all behind, whether they enjoy having an all-powerful kingdom or just find it a heavy burden, that they go without a moment's waiting, leaving their women and children behind?[40] That some people are very happy to go, and others sad and unwilling? Do you think there's anyone who can change that? Even a mighty king can do nothing in front of Yama's messenger. So who's going to listen to a poor woman? She, she's an orchard only God looks after.[41] What can she do about it? As for your Mahabharata, where does it show a woman going to ask Brahma if she could have her dead husband back, and being specifically told by Bhagavan the creator himself, 'No woman, whoever she is, can marry a second time in this life, once she's lost her first husband'? Apart from that one woman Savitri, no one has gone to Yama to try and get back her position as a wife. All right, so she went, and she got her husband back, and all sorts of other favours besides. So, even though this Savitri was only a woman, she dared to go to Yama's court to bring her husband back to life. Have you ever heard of a man who even set out on such a journey to save his wife's life, let alone one who got as far as she did? Once women have lost their position as wives, they have to hide their faces as if they've commited some huge crime worse even than murder and spend the rest of their lives shut away in a dark corner. So why don't you hide your faces when your wives have died, shave off your beards and moustaches and go off to live in the wilderness for the rest of your lives? Oh no, not you—one wife dies, and you just get another on the tenth day itself.[42] Just show us the evidence then—that some wise god has really told you to do this? In fact, what's good for a woman ought to be good for a man as well. What's so different about you? What—are you all such noble heroes that God gave you this freedom as a special gift?

Oh, you get your fine reputations from these so-called noble qualities—so long as no one examines them too closely! In fact, we women don't even need someone like the Rani of Jhansi to show us how: just take four or five hundred women who are free from attachments, put bayonets in their hands, then see what a time they'd give you.[43] You wouldn't even find a place to hide near the stove. In the old days of the Maratha kingdom, there really were heroes of the sword, those men who rocked the ancient throne of Delhi. But now since English rule came all your wonderful powers have gone, all your pleasures are ruined. Like the old saying—'No one's going to praise me, so I'll have to do it myself!'—so call yourselves heroes then, but only at pushing pens! Who takes any notice of you? Better still, with the way things are, it should be heroes at stuffing yourselves with food, that's the name that really suits you!

If you're so good pushing pens, so clever, pious, charitable, compassionate, if you're a real battislakshani[44] graced with all the virtues, how come you've got no love in you for your fellow creatures? Isn't there even a crumb of love in you? Or perhaps you've given it all out on loan—to the tigers in the jungle?

According to you, our own lives ought to give us a way of understanding the lives of others. What's happened to your lives here then? Isn't a woman's life as dear to her as yours is to you? It's as if women are meant to be made of something different from men altogether, made of the dust from earth or rock or rusted iron, whereas you and your lives are made from the purest gold. To you, woman is just some utterly trivial form of life, like a louse or a flea—and your own experience tells you that this is all very fine and good.[45] You're asking me what I mean? I mean once a woman's husband has died, not even a dog would swallow what she's got to. What's in store for her? The barber comes to shave all the curls and hair off her head, just to cool your eyes. All her ornaments are taken away. All her beauty vanishes. She's stripped and exposed in all sorts of ways as if she belonged to no one, she becomes the widow-pot hidden in the corner.[46] She's shut out from going to weddings, receptions and other auspicious occasions that married women go to. And why all these restrictions? Because her husband has died. She's unlucky: ill-fate is written on her forehead. Her face is not to be seen, it's a bad omen. She's a sign now for all these things. Oh, but her husband's died! All right, who says he hasn't? But was it she who killed him? Did she make some private prayer to God, 'God take this husband from me quickly?' In fact, she might very well have felt like asking God to take pity on her, praying, 'Take this husband quickly, Oh God, release me from this torture'. But then, she'd have stopped herself out of fear of the unhappiness she'd suffer after his lordship had gone. Who's to say? No—who'd think such a thought? It's like the old saying: 'Narayan did the deed, but it's Keshav does the penance!'[47] The husband's life is at an end, all finished. His good and bad points have all been added up and he's gone. But why should his wife take the blame for it? All right then, let's say that she should. But if she's supposed to give up everything after her husband's gone, and sit lamenting, 'Hari, Hari, god, Oh god', why shouldn't the man do the same? Why should he go off and marry another woman and settle down happily with her? Did the authors of the shastras keep their savage glares just for women? Maybe there was some woman once upon a time who went and set fire to their houses or something. So just because of this one woman, they went and invented a law and applied it to all women.

It would have been all right if a similar law had been imposed on all men at the same time. But would we ever get them to do that? They really used their heads, those authors of the shastras, when they made all this up. All very comfortable for them. Absolutely excellent! But what if they laid it down today that 'No man can remarry after his first wife has died. If he does, it's like he's committed incest with his mother and should be thrown out of caste?' And then the next day one of these chaps' own wives suddenly fell down dead. People would say even of him, 'He's got bad luck written on his forehead—we don't want to see his face'. It would be him who would be shut out as a guest at marriages and be thrown out of the village into a math.[48] So isn't it quite obvious that these men were just thinking of their own comforts when they gave men permission to marry any number of wives? Then their fortunes flourished! If one wife died or the poor thing got ill, then our chap just moves straight on to another. And if he happens to be a rich man as well, that's one more stroke of good luck on top of all the others. It means he enjoys two sorts of power: one comes from his money, and the other just because he's a man. There's nothing to hold him back!

You even get shrivelled up old sinners of eighty years or more, and there'll still be some oily-faced hanger-on who'll tell him, 'What nonsense, sir, who says you're old? If anyone dares say so, I'll push their teeth in'. 'But look,' the old man says, 'What about my hair? Doesn't that spoil it?' 'No, no—you just take a bit of this cream, sir, rub it on, and tomorrow it'll look fine, nothing to it!' 'Well, that's good, that's my hair fixed then. But my teeth—there's not a trace of one left in my head. Anything we could do about that, do you think?' 'No problem, my dear sir. Tomorrow I'll go along to a doctor I know who deals in teeth and I'll get you a brand new set, a full thirty-two. And next time you're washing your face, you just pull out any old bits of teeth still left and you'll be all ready, nothing to it. Even lads of twenty-five won't dare set themselves up alongside you. No, no, sir—these may be old bones, but does pepper ever fetch less than millet, even when it's a bit old and rotten?'[49] So it's all arranged and the old chap puffs up with pride, preening himself at the very thought. His few strands of hair on his bald head, his eyebrows and moustaches are all white, like bits of cotton wool, but he has his three rupee box of ointment brought to him and he rubs it in as instructed three times a day. Then he starts dressing himself up. He folds his dhoti and ties it up very tight. Then there's the turban with a gold border. And a shiny new jacket, which has to be forced on over his old bones. He finishes it off with a scarf over his shoulders and pops the borrowed set of teeth in his toothless mouth. Then he crushes up some betel for himself, to make his false teeth look good and red. Red sandals on his feet, and an imported walking stick in his hand in case he gets the shakes walking along. As for his diet, it's almond cakes, fried sweets, gourd sweets in syrup, ten times a day to fatten himself up. He inspects his ugly old face with its cheeks sunk in a hundred times in the mirror and struts about asking everyone, 'Well, hello there! How do you think I'm looking these days— pretty well, eh?' And then some mischief-maker will come along, and say, 'Tut, tut, sir, what's this about you being old? You don't look a day older than our Ganapati. You should find a wife! We don't have much fun at home these days ourselves, so how on earth do you manage? There's a saying, you know, 'Money troubles and you need relatives, but if it's diarrhoea a wife's best!'[50]

What next, then? The old man spends every minute of his time looking out for a woman, it's all he's got eyes for. Then it's done. The old corpse pays out a couple of thousand rupees and gets a pretty doe-eyed girl for himself, just like you buy a goat from the butcher and tie it up as bait to catch a tiger. Then out he goes one day and falls down dead, and it's all over. His worldly life is all finished and it's her again who's left to suffer. Right or not?

Do you ever find a woman going in for performances like these? Once the axe has fallen on her out of the sky, she accepts the burdens of widowhood, praises her husband's qualities good and bad and puts up with torments from the rest of the household till the day she dies. If a woman's husband has just a small illness her mouth dries up with terror. She watches him constantly, worrying for him more than her very life. It's out of devotion, you might say—or out of fear. She does everything just as he wishes. Of course, it's possible to be loving and open with someone, whether it's a man or a woman. But she has no choice but to be nice to him, however much she's got a mind of her own. So how can you tell her she's got to be all good and virtuous, when she just has to accept whatever you feel like handing out day after day? It's naturally from others that people learn how to behave, in good ways or bad. You can see this from your own experience. If you meet up with a cheat, isn't it likely you'll become a ten times bigger cheat yourself?

It's just the same in this case. There's a saying in English, that compassion breeds compassion. So just as compassion is born from the belly of compassion, you should start off by thinking what comes out of your own mind, then think what it does to others. But even this won't work where men are concerned. If a man's wife is ill for a year or two, then His Majesty will be saying, 'When's she going to die and get it over with?' or 'I'm just sick and tired of having to feed her medicine'. Whatever a wife's circumstances, she can't say anything like that, out of shame at what people would think. The husband, he's got to be treated with reverence no matter what happens. It's like the Muslims, whatever you are they find something grand to call you—if a man's wealthy, he's an amir, if he's poor, he's a fakir and after he's died, they call him a pir![51] A man who isn't married is given the title of brahmachari; those who are married are called householders and family men.[52] Then, when a man's been through all the stages of life, he gives up the world and becomes a sanyasi, and that's the end! But what's the proper

.time of day for people to take the vow of sanyas? It's in the evening.[53] But you—you don't give up these worldly hopes till the very last moment, when the doctors have given up all hope of your life. Then and only then you'll take the vow to become a sanyasi, at some unearthly hour in the morning!

What a cunning lot of jackals you are then, real experts at it! If only God would preserve this English government forever! Since it began here, women have got the gift of education, and their minds made strong enough to face all sorts of mental and practical circumstances with courage. The ignorance that made its home in their hearts is all gone and they've begun to get some understanding of what's good for them and what isn't, of how they should behave to whom, of how they can best drive on this cart that's our life in the world; they have begun to get some understanding of truth, of dharma, of pativrata. Because of all this, things are going to change a lot in this land of Bharat. But there are some people who are enemies of women to their very bones, like the Pune Vaibhav newspaper. These people hate all the new things, or so it seems from one or two articles in the newspaper. These must have been appearing continually now for the last four or five months. Some widow by name of Vijaylakshmi got herself an abortion, or she might have had the child and sent it off to heaven herself—enquiries are going on about that at the moment.[54] So someone took up the poor widow's cause and wrote a letter to the government, saying widows ought to be married again. Then his lordship editor of the Vaibhav got into a furious rage over this and shouted his head off: 'The English government shouldn't ever put its hand in our religion!' But actually he's no different from all the other men. He doesn't look like a real reformer but he is one all the same, it's just that his reforms are all disguised. If you look at it, what religious differences are left now between European people and our own? There's only one difference left, and if you ask what, it's that people won't marry or have other sorts of physical connection with the women of another caste. That's all that's left now. For the rest, what customs of European people are there that you haven't taken on for yourselves?

You've started to wear clothes like theirs. You've made yourselves as learned as they are, if not more. You enjoy the things they eat to your hearts' content, like meat and alcohol. You keep . on trying to be just like them, yet you go on about them not putting

their hands in our religion! But how much of this religion is there
left now? You go wherever you like in trains and boats, you dress
just like them—a jacket on your back, a hat on your head, trousers,
socks and shoes, a little handkerchief sprinkled with lavender
water in your hand, a pipe in your mouth to finish it off. You turn
yourselves into real live sahibs (the only difference being that
they're white all over, and you're half white and half black, like a
piebald horse!). You eat all sorts of forbidden foods just as your
fancy takes you, you do all sorts of improper things, then you turn
round and claim you're great defenders of dharma. Aren't you even
slightly ashamed saying it?

Then you get into steamships, don't you, and go off to
countries where there isn't a single member of your own caste. You
mix with those people and spend year after year close in company
with them. Then you just come back here, do a panchagavya
penance, then there you are, all ready and proud to take your place
at the communal table once more![55]

So you think that makes it all right, do you? But can you really
wash out those intestines of yours which are stuffed full of things
you shouldn't have eaten, by taking baths and special penances and
rubbing cows' urine on your body? Why all these tears for your
religion? In fact, wouldn't it be a far better way of defending our
religion if the government did put its hand in and stopped you
spending all that money on endless bottles of drink, and all those
thousands of poor chickens and other birds and beasts being killed
for you to eat? I quite agree with the old proverb that says, 'A
stranger steps in, and harm comes to the house', and I would have
followed it in what I did if you hadn't taken on a single one of these
people's habits, if you'd followed your own dharma to the letter.[56]
Even the poor widows would have realized that their fortunes were
never going to get better and would have kept quiet. But all that
Manu, it's changed and gone now.[57] What's left of it? Those people
are just better than you a thousand times over. Do they copy a
single one of our people's customs on these worthless whims? Just
the opposite, they look at these get-ups of yours and laugh. Oh,
you asses, if someone from a distant land or one of your forefathers
came back again to see, they wouldn't even be able to recognize
this place. All these different arts and skills have come in the last
fifty years and everything has changed, and if you came back like
the black sheep in the family, you'd see what a change there's been!

You ask what? In places where you always used to be able to hear the pothis and puranas, it's all alphabets being recited. Then people used to furnish their homes in the old way, as suited their different ranks. They used to use woollen rugs, stuffed cushions for leaning on, pillows for sitting on, little stools and suchlike, other bits of furniture. For pots and pans, there used to be our little metal pots and plates, brass lamps, torches made of oil-soaked pieces of cloth. Instead of this, now we have chairs, couches and tables; instead of our own utensils, there are cups and saucers, knives, scissors, spoons, kerosene lamps, lamps shaped like the moon, reading lamps. Instead of the old vada houses, the verandahs and inner courtyards have gone and it's all bungalows instead.[58] All right then, let's go out outside; perhaps your old relative might be able to recognize the place from some of the old things. But you won't recognize anything from people's clothes any more. You ask how so? If you look at men's turbans for instance, they're now just tied according to any old caste rule, or people wear hats, or just some long black or white piece of cloth put on any old way. Ten or twenty years ago, who'd have wound such tatty old strips of cloth round their heads like that, apart from Telugu folk or people in mourning?[59] In those days, you used to be able to tell from what people wore on their heads that this man is a Telugu, or that one has just had a death in the family. But now you see ranks of such turbans wherever you look, and half-jackets and coats, and watches with swinging chains. So how can you tell who a man is? If you look down, he has trousers on his legs, and boots and stockings. Is he a Muslim, or a Parsi, or some Sahib's cook? You'll have to go and ask him who he is, won't you?

So much for clothes. You're always hanging round their offices, so go on, dress like them if you like. But do you think your silly childish faces look right in those clothes? They look all right on people if they're white. But when some fellow who's black as coal puts them on, it just looks like a strange disguise. That's the funny thing about dress. Drink is another funny thing. A sahib generally makes one bottle do for a couple of days. But our fellow seems to need a bottle a minute, as well as a brace of pigeons for supper. And then he'll turn up shouting what a champion of dharma he is, and how we don't want anyone else stepping in amongst us. What should we say to someone like that?

Look now, these people brought to your country and your

people the skills which each of them needed. They showed you how to be human. You were human before that all right, but absolutely ignorant and stupid, just like savage demons. All you knew was you hit me and I'll hit you. There were revolts and rebellions in the Maratha kingdom then. These people put an end to them and spent crores of rupees giving you education. They brought all sorts of arts and skills, all kinds of laws and regulations; they set up offices and courts and protected everyone in peace and comfort. They broke open mountains and laid down tracks for the trains to move along, great broad chariots of fire. At one time or other, in the ancient time of the Dvaparayuga, people built caves at places like Verul, Ajanta, Karle, and Nasik—those are the ones I know of, but there are hundreds of thousands of caves deep in the earth.[60] People these days say that the Pandavas carved them out, while they were wandering in hiding. But has anyone ever seen the Pandavas, or Draupadi? These rulers though, they're real Pandavas. In pothis, in the Ramavijay, Shridhar Swami has written that Indrajit made an offering of fire to the gods and so built a chariot of fire for himself.[61] But that chariot couldn't have carried countless heavy weights like the ones we have now, and taken them like the wind to specified places and at specified times. These are just a few of all the different strange marvels you could describe. Just try going out at night now, carrying a load of silver on your back—you'll have nothing to fear. This government has done so much to promote your happiness. If they don't reach in and change this religion of ours, make women who are weak strong and rescue them from this sham dharma and all the misery it makes—if they don't, who will?

This editor of the Vaibhav says the laws the government has passed so far are only the thin end of the wedge. So from what he writes it's you men who are traitors and disloyal. 'If we give up shaving widows' heads, the government will start building hundreds of homes for prostitutes to live in like Bavanakhani, and have to set up all sorts of new courts to try crowds of cases like Vijaylakshmi's.'[62] In fact, instead of building more quarters for prostitutes, we'd be much more likely to find the government building a neat little house for each one of them, and a great prison house to put people like you in. You're asking how? Well, say the government made it possible for women to remarry. Then each and every one of those women, living happily with their new husbands in the little kingdom of their homes, would become the firm and lifelong supporters of the British government. Then the government could collect up all those tigers and goats of men, with their swollen lusts, with their minds fuddled with drink and their bellies stuffed with meat, and stick them in a big strong prison. It could save itself a lot of money by putting all these animals to work, instead of the poor bullocks, buffaloes, horses and donkeys who have to suffer pain from hard work at present. If the government did this, it could fill its treasury and get merit at the same time!

A father and mother make you the gift of their daughter once and for all, they pour the water over your hands and that's the end of it.[63] Then she leaves and she's lost to them. Oh, the pity of it—from the day of her birth, the father and mother have followed their natural feelings and raised her up from child to adult with praise and love, each as best they could. See how hard they've worked to get her a place that's good and happy, to please her new family of in-laws in the hope they'll love her and treat her kindly. If good luck's on her side, everything's fine. But what if it isn't? All her life long, her mother and father have cherished her, dear as life itself.[64] What must it be like for her, whose father and mother never gave her the lightest slap, when she feels the sharp blows of your fist on her back? What must her parents feel? If I wrote down the raw truth it would fill up a book as big as the Ramayana. And when you do treat a woman well, it's usually only just for show. You're like someone who wears a wonderful bit of red and gold silk brocade on his top half, and a tattered old blanket below. You can even cover her with gold ornaments and put her in a house set with jewels. But if you're not kind and loving, she'll still feel nothing but misery—misery which you can't just describe, you have to experience it.

Women in this world are forever putting up with all sorts of hard toil, difficulty, hunger and thirst, harassment and beatings—and all they ask is a kindly word from you. It's true, you go out and earn the money. But she has to see to the running of the house, has to do exactly as you tell her, perpetually obedient, kept in ignorance, toiling at the most exhausting work till her body's pleasure breaks into little pieces, her bones waste away and her blood turns to water—her eyes always on your face. You've only got to glance at her approvingly and flash your teeth in a smile, and she feels it's a joy divine! This encourages her to take up the burden of labour again, to learn and do even more kinds of work.[65] Look at it from what you know already. There's a saying of yours, 'A husband's praise is like nectar and ambrosia'. Let's say she brings some beautiful piece of sewing to show you, or serves up a nicely prepared little delicacy, and you tell her 'Well, now, look at this! Did you really make it yourself? Look now, don't work so hard! You'll give yourself backache; you might hurt your eyes. We don't want the children to suffer for it, and we must keep you out of the hands of the doctor! You just take it easy now'. Or if you're with your friends and you say, 'You know, I'm so lucky, I don't have to worry about anything at home. Let's just go off to my place and do something there. It'd be hard to find a home as good as ours'. As soon as she hears these words of love and praise, she forgets all the pain she's suffered since childhood, all the times that you've kicked and punched and sworn at her. With this praise from her lord and master, she tells herself she's the luckiest person on earth. Her heart overflows with affection. So there she is, eagerly looking to you for the smallest sign of love—and you still go on calling her all sorts of insulting names. There's no denying it—this is what her fate really is.

As for you gods—why do you do these strange things?[66] Does anyone understand? Look, a woman spends all her life with someone domineering over her, like a bought slave. She has to calculate her husband's pleasure all the time, as if with tiny goldsmiths' scales, bear up under the heaviest work in the house, suffer whatever the family says to her. Sometimes she toils like a hired bullock; other times she's like a doe, worrying herself day and night about the house and family.[67] When she does all this, can't a woman have power to speak even one word, or have even a pinch of grain to call her own?[68] So tell us Vidhatya, what record of destiny have you stamped on her? If you're going to do such things to her why didn't you just kill her as soon as she was born? Wouldn't that have saved you getting thousands of curses from women today?[69]

Oh yes, it's blessings all round for them that you gods look after—always after freedom for your own kind! What is it makes you so keen to keep women shut up? Maybe it's because even you've got the pride of men and their kind?

You're gods, aren't you? Your door's open the same to everyone, no favouritism this way or that—so what's all this now?

In fact, aren't you the very fathers of all favouritism? Wasn't it you who created women just like you did men? So why did you hand out happiness to one and misery to the other? Baba, what a mistake you made. But it's women who suffer the consequences—oh yes, they suffer all right.

We read about all the faults women are supposed to have, and hear about them as we go about our daily business. But haven't men got any of these faults themselves? Is it that women tell lies and men don't? What about stealing, whoring, murder, robbery, trickery, taking government money in bribes, making lies into truth, and truth into lies—don't men do any of this? There's a lot written about women in that chapter where Kaikeyi tells Dasaratharaj, 'You send Ramchandra off into the jungle for fourteen years and put my son Bharat on the throne of Ayodhya instead'.[70] But the men of those days, of the Satyayuga, they really did care about the truth. Once they'd promised, they never shifted. Harischandra gave his kingdom to a brahman in a dream and Vishvamitra persecuted him horribly. Shibiraj cut the flesh off from his own body for the dove and put it in scales to be weighed. Raja Yavanashva kept faith by giving his living body to Shrikrishna Paramatma Dvarkadhish to be cut in half with a saw.[71] Similarly, Dasaratharaj sent Ramchandra into the wilderness on Kaikeyi's orders, which he regarded as the essence of truth. That was how men used to stand up for the truth. People in those days used to yield to three kinds of will: of women, of children and of kings. But in today's circumstances there's only one, and that's rulers. Children can still be wilful about things too. But women can't get their way any more, I don't see how they can. If any of them tries, she loses the skin off her back with a beating, a ration enough to make her remember it for six months or a year. This is what happens when women try being wilful about anything now.[72] So who's going to try? You see what happened to one woman's back and that's enough. Let's just take one verse here, and you'll see the essence of it.

ovi

Woman is only the axe, that cuts down trees of virtue

Hindrance to creatures through thousands of births

Know her to be the temptress, embodiment of pains in this world.[73]

sloka

A whirlpool of changing whims, a house of vice, a city of
                                                    shamelessness
   A mine of faults, a region of deceit, a field of distrust
Obstacle at heaven's door, mouth of hell's city, well of evil magic
Who made this woman-device, sweet poison and trap of all
                                                    creatures ?[74]

So this is what you do—you heap all your contempt on
women's heads, so it's you who become the very image of virtue!
    If women really do cut down the tree of your virtue like an axe,
how come you value this creature more than life itself, the very axe
supposed to destroy your lives? Why do you take the care of her
under your own lifelong control and put her to work like a bullock
in every possible daily chore? In fact, even bullocks are better than
you. At least they can look after themselves. But let all this be.
    So the first point.[75] If there's a force greater than evil incanta-
tions in that device of women, you're stronger than her when it
comes to brains. Is there anything you haven't done with those
great brains of yours, a single monstrous deed in the world you
haven't committed? What strength have women got next to you
and your huge power? They've got nothing at all.
    In the second place, it's true women are whirled about by many
whims! But it's because they're uneducated that every kind of
whim makes its home in their minds. Even so, theirs only go as far
as their own families. But if we look at your minds, all the whims
there go round so fast we can hardly see them. Your minds are
constantly churned up with all sorts of cunning schemes, to do
with things native and foreign, imaginary and practical. Today you
might say, perhaps we should trick some moneylender and fleece
him of a thousand rupees. We could pass information to a
particular jagirdar and take him for four or five hundred. I know,
you'll say, today let's tell the sahib such and such, and get that case
decided on some chap's behalf. Another day, and it's 'Maybe we
should bring along that false title-deed for copying and entry'. But
do you ever find women scheming, 'That woman, you know, she
acts so superior—you'd think she had to peel onions with her
nose! We ought to set a trap for the little snob and get rid of her
for good!' Whims like this never even come into women's minds.
All women on this earth don't shine as brightly as the light of the

sun, of course not. Nor are they all purer than Ganges water inside
and out. But if you added up all the women in the world, you'd
find only ten in a hundred with minds going round and round like
yours, when there isn't a single one of you that's free from it.

Thirdly, then: that women are the very abode of debauchery.
You think your kind are better, do you? If you weighed it up, the
scales would sink down a hundred, a hundred and a half times
heavier on your side.

In the fourth place, the idea that women are a very city of thoughtlessness.[76] But does thoughtlessness only come from women's hands?
And you, who are mean and faithless, who make promises to others
then cut their throats behind a mask of kindness—are you never
thoughtless? Oh yes, you're absolute temples of thought, let's congratulate you! You're meant to be so wonderfully learned and thoughtful, but you've actually committed acts of thoughtlessness like we've
never seen before, and so you carry on every day. Yet you call yourselves such great thinkers—so I wonder what we should call you?

Women are ignorant, just like female buffaloes in a pen. They
may not be able to read or write, but does that mean God never
gave them any intelligence at all? They may be thoughtless, but
they're still much better than you. You men are all very clever, it's
true. But you just go and look in one of our prisons—you'll find it
so stuffed full of your countrymen you can hardly put your foot on
the ground. Oh yes, they're all very clever there, aren't they? One's
there for making counterfeit notes, another for taking bribes,*

---

* Just look at this—the government pays you to do its work honestly.
Depending on your talents and education it pays you anything from ten to a
hundred rupees a month and sometimes even more: two hundred, three, four,
five, six, a thousand or more. It puts complete trust in you, you say all right, you
both agree, and it puts you to work just signing bits of paper. What's wrong
with that? But you, even though you're paid for the job, you don't hesitate to
take all sorts of other things on top of it, from rich and poor alike: ready cash,
horses, cows, buffaloes, cloth, silver, pots, and if people have nothing else to
give, even their shoes. Doesn't this make you the most faithless traitors? Oh, if
you can't get anything else you'll even take a day's food. From one person,
you'll take a guava or two sticks of sugar cane, from another a bit of jaggery or
just sticks of wood, from a third even a few grains of millet and from a fourth
you just steal! Is there anyone you let go without this pretence at alms-giving,
or till they've bared their teeth in a smile? Come on, you know the answer's
never! With you it's always begging and demanding. Oh, if we began to
describe all these so-called virtues of yours we'd never find enough room for all
the paper. We'd have the whole universe filled up with paper, we'd have to dry
up all the seas to make ink and employ a carpenter specially to sharpen the pens!

another for running off with someone else's wife, another for taking part in a rebellion, another for poisoning, another for treason, another for giving false evidence, another for setting up as a raja and destroying the people, yet another for doing a murder. Of course, it's these great works of thought that make the government offer you a room so reverently in its palatial prisons! What women do things like these? How many prisons are filled with women? For every two or three thousand of you, you won't find even a hundred women. If we ask ourselves what's the worst thoughtlessness women can be guilty of, it would be adultery— that's the peak of Meru here.[77] But whoever caused it should get the blame. When a woman gets into adultery, who is it who takes the first steps by planting bad desires in her mind? Her or you? However shameless a woman might be, she'll never force her arms round a man's neck, that's for certain. Because what's the greatest happiness in the world for a woman? In the first place, it's a husband who suits her and really loves her. If he and she are of one mind, she can be ever so poor, live in a hut short of food and clothes, put up with all sorts of suffering and trouble, go off and live in the jungle—but she'll still only have eyes for one man and regard all her trials as happiness.[78] Left to herself a woman would never turn to adultery.

Of course, it isn't true that women in the past have never done it. Take the shastras, whose power you all talk so big about. We don't have the same mess and muddle now, but if a king died then without a direct heir, his queen could prolong the line with whichever of the sages she fancied. And her majesty would keep him on the job, wouldn't she, till she'd got not one but ten sons. What was going on there, then? Wasn't that illicit sex? Wasn't that adultery? Is that what the shastras agree with? In fact, if it had been possible for a woman to get married again properly this whole kingdom would be much more powerful. Our country wouldn't be impoverished like it is today, with thousands of little kingdoms, jagirs, inams, deshmukhis and so on all disappearing. Many of these didn't have proper heirs, so all their estates went and fell into the government treasury. In some places people shaved all the women's heads who were left, and because no one was there to see their troubles, you fell on them like a swarm of locusts and clean wiped them out. Oh, there were women as beautiful as nymphs in the courts of those kings, women whose feet had never even touched the dirt on the ground, but your covetous designs made paupers and vagrants of them.[79] Would they have suffered such misery if they'd been free to marry again? They never would have. When a husband has died that's one life gone, stone-dead. But just because of that, another four, five, even ten lives get wrecked. See, if one wife doesn't have a son, the number of wives just keeps growing, a seond, a third, fourth, and on it goes. Among Marathas and Deshmukhs each man can have four or five wives, three at the very least, and no one says anything. Then one day the old boy sets out on his road to heaven, and every one of his wives has to sit there banging her forehead, sons or not. Women's minds are very soft. They're easily satisfied—unlike you, their heads aren't always buzzing with ideas about how to get important jobs and money. They're not always worrying, 'Do people respect me properly? Or just talk about "that old Gomaji"?' It isn't women who spend their whole lives trying to get what they can't have. So what should we say, when you turn round and lay the whole weight of blame on women for being thoughtless?

The fifth point, then—that women are the storehouse of all guilt. In fact, it's the other way round—when women go wrong it's always because of you. See now. Many fathers marry off their daughters of ten or eleven, girls who shine like little stars, they marry them for a fat wad of rupees to some rich old man of eighty or ninety.[80] They eye the old man's wealth and say, 'Well—it won't really matter if he does die, will it? She'll never want for money, after all. In a couple of days, she'll be back to eating and drinking, putting on ornaments, dressing as usual and so on. What does it matter if there's no husband?' With words like that they hand her over shamelessly, like a goat to the tiger. Oh, but the husband has gone who would have been her real happiness and love, who would have taken pleasure in her ornamenting and dressing up, who would have praised her and cherished her more than life itself. With him gone, the whole world is just a wilderness to her. What's the point of this empty ceremony for her? In the old days, a woman used to go as sati*—that was good. She could turn herself to ashes along with him, and it was all over with.[81]

---

* You know there's the Sarvajanik Sabha at Pune.[82] They did women such a great favour. In that publication of theirs that comes out every six months or so, someone took it upon themselves to ask very pompously, 'Whether it

Apart from her mother, no one will ever love her as much as a husband, that's certain. When she's lost both, where's she going to get strength to pull on through her days, with the flaming coals of youth burning in her breast? This is the position of girls given away just for money.

Some people give away their daughters as second wives. But there's no weapon that pierces a woman so painfully as the thorn of being given as second wife. A wife's blood boils if her husband just looks a bit closely at another woman. And that's just looking. So how can she bear it if he goes and marries someone else, or takes another woman on the side, whether it happens inside the house or not? You'll never ever find two women living happily in the same house. You can treat them as equally as you like in things like jewellery and clothes. But how can you love two in the same way as one? Love isn't like a mango or a guava—you can't cut it up and share it out. Love is like milk. Once it's gone sour, you can't make it good again, no matter how much you stir it about. Once it's separated, you can't put it back together. Yes, it's only natural for people to prefer new things over the old, it doesn't matter who it is. But a man's wife has only to look at someone else with a bit of interest and he'll work himself up into the most furious rage. Then her family has to suffer in disgrace and she gets beaten, locked up and harassed. Why doesn't any of this apply to you?

If you can't bear her just looking, will she stand it when it feels like a burning pan right on her chest? Why do people give their girls away as second wives? If someone has lots of daughters, often they'll just give them to any husband that comes along. It doesn't matter what he's like—some push their daughters off onto a man who'll quite plainly destroy his family. A man can be as ugly as you

---

would be good or not, if government allowed women to go as sati?' But when women have gone as sati, why do you hang back making cowdung cakes for the fire?[83] Why shouldn't you go as sati when your wives have died? Much more harm is done from her going instead of you—she leaves little children behind her, and who's going to look after them?

There's a saying, isn't there, 'Let the father die, out galloping horses, but the mother mustn't, who sits spinning at her wheel'. If the father dies, the mother may grieve or not, it all depends. But she still takes care of the children. If she fell down dead today though, you'd just go out tomorrow and find yourself another wife, then the children would be turned out on the streets. Isn't that right? There's someone making a fuss about cases like this every day of the week. So it's you who should be thrown into the pot first, not women.

like, full of vices, pitiless and cruel, fond of beating and harassing,
who'll even keep his family short of food and drink. But people still
give their girls to such bringers of misery, handing them over like
cows to a butcher.[84] A whole cartload of paper wouldn't be enough
if I tried to describe it all here. So whose fault is it then, if women
run away because of it? The father's or the daughter's?

In fact, you'll find very few women, when they have that
greatest of all happiness—a husband that suits them—who'll still
go ahead and do these bad things just to get jewels and ornaments
or pleasure. Now, perhaps you'll point to the example of a king's
family and say that there, at least, there could be no lack of
happiness. But do they take their wives along with them in their
retinues? It's hard to make kings and other great rich people do
anything. For six months of the year, they don't even set eyes on
their queens and wives at home, so the women have no pleasures at
all. What are they supposed to do? There they are, surrounded by
luxury and comfort, food and drink all provided for. How can the
men hold them back, these flowers? It's like the saying, 'Mother
won't feed them, and father won't let them go out and beg'.[85]
When you get this happening to women, then of course they'll end
up like sows, rooting around in the filth.[86] This is just one example.
But actually, it's you men who make them go wrong. What reason
would they have for doing these things, if you'd only stick to a
promise of one wife? Now for another example. Some women
deceive their husbands when they have every comfort and happiness. But what are the circumstances here? There you are, reciting
the entire list of a woman's praises over and over in her ear, making
a great show of your passion, calling her your queen and mistress,
telling her you're her slave, her bondsman, her servant. Give me
just one loving look you say, I hunger for just one word from you,
I'll be the garland round your neck, I'll do anything you want. I'll
put you in a palanquin, your feet won't touch the dirt on the
ground, I'll go round carrying your shoes in my mouth. You go on
and on imploring her, and the poor woman drinks in all your false
promises as if they were nectar—and so she takes the jump.[87]

Here you might ask, why does she jump into it when she can
see what's happened to other women who have cheated and can
get an idea of what her own troubles will be? You'd need God
himself nearby to have enough control of mind. Because the sex-
urge is so strong, isn't it? Even people who call themselves the very

ocean of wisdom. Aren't they always pushing forward with all sorts of bold wild schemes, eh?[88] If we did live in a world where a mistake once made was never repeated, the government wouldn't be paying for lakhs of people to be kept and fed in prison.

What great thugs you are, then—you don't even let lightning out of your grasp, so what's a bit of wife-stealing to you? True, it takes two hands to clap, but the right hand's still the strongest.

There are some rich gentlemen so fond of their daughters that they marry them to a boy from a poor family, so they can have the pair close to them at home.[89] Everything goes along nicely, just as long as both are simple and ignorant—but then the woman begins to get a bit of experience. She's from a wealthy home, used to being kept in comfort and luxury, bright and intelligent; and her husband has been nothing but a poor wretch all his life. His father never knew what comfort was, nor intelligence. The boy might be able to get some idea, using his natural talents. But how's he going to learn the proper way to behave for someone who's rich and grand? He's been poor from birth and known nothing but a poor man's food. You can get hold of a common donkey and brush him down twice a day, feed him pounds of grain, put a saddle on him embroidered with gold and silver, a plume of feathers and a pair of silver silk tassels at his tail. But even after all this decoration, would he be able to stand up next to a proper horse, even a skinny broken down old nag? So the woman takes a dislike to him—it's as if someone's patched a fine shawl with a dirty bit of old blanket. And what happens after that is just what you'd expect—I don't want to show all that here! People get laughed at and taunted for it every day, we can see it with our own eyes. Why can't a father make his love useful to her all her life long instead? If he'd only arrange a suitable husband for her in the first place, he could get great pleasure from seeing them both flourishing and happy.

You wouldn't like to be stuck with some oaf of a wife who was nasty, ugly, vicious and filthy, would you? Why should a wife like it any better? Doesn't she want a good husband, just like you want a good wife? Oh, when you were little, your father and mother were poor as beggars, but poor as they were they still took great pains over their son's marriage. They borrowed money and got themselves into debt, but somehow or other they fixed up a marriage for you. At that time of course, there was no chance of a girl at all good or beautiful. You could have got a real scarecrow

and you'd have still thought she was a nymph. Then you get
blessed with a bit of education and promoted to some important
new office—and you start feeling ashamed of your first wife.
Money works its influence on you and you begin to say to yourself,
what does a wife matter after all? Don't we just give them a few
rupees a month and keep them at home like any other servant, to
do the cooking and look after the house? You begin to think of her
like some female slave you've paid for—a thousand, twelve
hundred rupees down, and now it's me who owns her. You love your
favourite dog or horse more than you ever do your wife. What's a
wife, after all? She's just like the alley or the cowshed at the back of
the house—why should anyone bother about her or trouble to ask
how she is? If one of your horses died it wouldn't take long to
replace it, and there's no great labour needed to get another wife
either. You lose one, you get another. If it's a poor man he looks
after her a bit, because he knows if she dies he'll have a hard job
finding another. But the rich don't even do this much. They'd get
married to someone different every day of the week if they could.
The problem is Yama hasn't got time to carry off wives fast
enough, or you'd probably get through several different ones in
one day! But anyway, it nearly chokes you to have to say to people,
this is my wife. No one ever used courtesies when they spoke to
you before—but now you've got the force of offices and money
behind you, so people start calling you Appasahib this, Babasahib
that.[90] So you get the idea you should have a new wife to go with it
and start looking forward impatiently to your wedding day. Does a
wife ever treat people like this? Doesn't she just try to obey you
and please you, whether times are good or bad? Does a wife ever
say to herself, 'He's got no money and he's ugly too, I think I'll go
off with someone else'? Whose crimes are worst, then: women's or
men's?

    Now for the sixth point. Which of us is really soaked a hundred
times over in deceit? You're number one here. How can we
describe your deceit? Every step and there's an example. Look at
all the disguises you get yourself up in—you could even paint your
body black and yellow striped and change into a tiger. You turn
yourselves into gosavis, fakirs, haridasas, brahmacharis, sadhus,
dudharais, giripuris, bharatis, nanaks, kanphotas, jogis, jatadharis,
nanges, you pretend you've renounced the whole world, smear
ashes on your bodies, grow your hair matted and go off to live in

the jungle—you go round deceiving all the world with your tricks. Who's that, it's a ramgiribuva, that one a shastribuva, another parades as Ganpatibuva Phaltankar the great sadhu, another as a nanakpanthi. What qualities they all have![91] What can we say? They've got all the proper merits, they're so detached, they hand out holy mantras. They only have to tell us and we believe them. As the buva's fame spreads he takes to stuffing himself with rich delicacies and grows sleek and shiny like a tomcat, then somehow his religious duties get forgotten. He sits there as the women come to take his darshan and prays on very different beads. He picks out some specially who are young and freshly nubile, and there he sits, meditating and repeating to himself, this one's nice, that one's pretty! Not a word about your Shiva or Hari, they're all forgotten! The only name on his lips is that girl's, who looks just like the milkmaid Radha.[92] The only thing he's got eyes for is that fresh young flower's pretty laughing face, and inside it's Mr Money he's meditating on![93] He might look as though he's crazy—but it's crazy like a fox!

Then who's this coming along? It's a brahmachari fresh from Kashi. So majestic, this buva, it's a very god who stands before us with folded hands. And look what he's got along with him—a palanquin, a carriage, a dozen spirited horses, and a band of ten or twelve disciples as fresh and glossy as the horses. One says he's Gangadas, another says he's Ramprasad. Gangadas doesn't need teaching how to sing his master's praises: 'Really, our Maharaj has had a vision of God. Some time back the headman of Ujad village hadn't a single child. Then he gave him some holy ashes and he got a son, he really is something special! There have been people with diseases, people afflicted by evil spirits. It's enough for them just to take his darshan and it's gone. Yes, he's Sambha's avatar all right!'[94] Once one person has talked, the world needs no lessons how to spread it. First it's just a feather, then they're talking about a crow and on it goes. And the buva struts about so importantly, so pompous on the outside—but if anyone could look inside, they'd just see two scorching flames of desire, for women and wealth.

Oh yes, you put strings of sacred tulsi beads around your necks, you go round reciting the virtues of Viththal, posing as servants of Hari, famous beggars, you take yourselves off to Kashi.[95] But do you think you can wipe it all clean by going off there and shaving your beard and moustaches as penance?

You can offer up your moustaches and throw them on the waters of the Bhagirathi, but do you think you can bundle up your vices and do the same with them?[96] Of course you can't—that way you only get more pride and bad desires. Outside you make as if you're the holiest of holy men—but can even Bhagirathi's waters put out the flaming torch of deceit inside you?

So, you take the sanyasi vow, do you? Then you should give up all your hopes and desires. There you are, with your saffron robes, your staff and water-pot in your hand, honouring all the world and its creatures like Narayan himself. But let's look at what happens on the banks of the Ganges, when you're washing and purifying yourself on the beautiful stone steps, smearing pound after pound of ashes on your body, sitting there repeating the name, Paramatma Sheshashayi Shrinarayan, and telling prayer beads with the gomukhi on your hand.[97] When your ears catch the sound of feet on the first step of the ghat, your eyes dart up, the glove falls from your hand, our buva's thrown into confusion and Narayan runs right out of his mouth. What sort of a Narayan is it coming now? It's one in the form of a woman, and now it's she who goes and sits in the buva's gomukhi. 'Outside they parade in saffron robes; inside the ulcer of evil thoughts'. Who really sees what's going on? It's collect money from alms and off to a whore with it—that's what abandoning the world means here!

The gods themselves bring destruction on women, so is it any wonder you do the same? When Krishna got Arjuna to disguise himself as a big holy man and steal Subhadra away, the Yadavas' sons said to each other 'A holy man's carried Aunty off!'[98] But do you ever hear of the aunt carrying off the holy man? There was the time when no one could stand up against Ravana and he went about harassing all the three worlds. Everywhere people were crying and groaning, Indrapur was deserted and the gods and rishis went running to Sheshashayi Bhagavan at Kshirasagar, shouting for pity, 'Stop that devil tormenting us and making us his slaves'.[99] That all-powerful god could raise the whole world or destroy it in an instant, just as he wished. What was Ravana worth against that infinite power? But that isn't how people interpret it now. Ravana stole Sita away, so the monkey army had to go after them to his kingdom in the south and destroy it—that was what really happened. But now people say, 'Oh, never mind all that other stuff; it was that whore who really ruined Ravana. See what these wretched women get up to, destroying homes and kingdoms'.

What have we got, then? It's all women's fault again. Sita even took the fire ordeal, but people still went on blaming her.[100] Did that make Ramchandra all the greater or something? What wonderful gods you've got! You're the shadows of them: they show up once, but you really show up double. How can we tell about this deceit of yours? There's one of you pretending to be just like a brother to someone, and all the time secretly hoping something bad will happen to him; another who pretends to be like a father, and really hopes his friend will suffer a loss; and another of you who makes as if he's a true friend, and all the while his eye's on everything from his friend's wife to his dog. Hardly any men are pure outside as well as in. Five or six of you characters get together and then what? 'That chap, you know, he really flashes his money around, it'd be good to see his nose pulled down for once!' Or: 'That fellow's done all right for himself, what a marvel! He never even used to get enough to eat, but now that son of a whore rides round in a two horse buggy!' That's work to you—you're like a lot of crows, heads full of dirty tricks and you're pecking holes in other people for their secret follies. Tell us then, go on—do women ever do that? Has a woman ever dressed up as a gosavi or sadhu and got a man to run away with her? Show us, then, if you can find even one single example?

Women are so covetous and gullible by nature they'll believe anything they're told. There's no saying what they'll do to get children, riches and love from their husbands. An example of that was a story recently in a newspaper of a woman who had no sons, and some mischievous fraud of a priest told her she'd get pregnant if she got hold of a little boy's you-know-what, mixed it with jaggery and ate it. She found a suitable opportunity and took the fine medicine. Then it all got out and made a big scandal, and her husband got a stick and really softened up her back with it, so she killed herself to avoid public disgrace.

Now, that woman would never have put her hand to such a scheme if she'd had some education. There are all kinds of these tricksters, joshis, kanphotas, bairagis, who lead women on and deceive them with promises that they'll be able to win all their husbands' love for themselves and keep them how they want forever. 'You'll get a boy if you look at a house where there are children on a Saturday night when there's a full moon, then light a fire'. 'Choose a Saturday night when there's no moon, wash your hair, put a broken pot on your head, then come out without any

clothes on and take a darshan at eleven temples of Maruti'.[101]
Women listen to these false promises and put instant faith in them.
They only do these reckless things in the hope of having sons and
keeping their husbands' affection. Women's minds are so trusting
they enter into things very readily no matter how hard the tasks. So
it's quite clear how ignorant and thoughtless they are. But it would
only be fair to blame them if they were as sharp and clever as you,
had all the good things you enjoy and still went on doing it.

Now, if it's allure you want to talk about, certainly women are
the very embodiment of it, head to toe. Their every limb, their
voices, their ways of walking and talking and doing their work—at
every step they're the loadbearers of other people's desires. But is it
a woman's fault if men act like bees round a honeycomb, greedy
with desire just at the sight of her?[102]

You just try this: take a huge cooking pot, fill it with gold coins
and stand a woman next to it. Then bring along a great sadhu, a
brahmachari, and say to him: 'Now, sir, choose which you like
best, and take it'. Then see if he doesn't throw the pot of gold aside
and stretch out his hands towards the other gold, the lovely woman.

Now for the seventh point, that women are the beginning of all
wickedness. No—wickedness starts off with you and you alone.
You desert your own dharma and carry on just as you please,
getting drunk and rolling in the road, going round looking at
young boys in tamashas, gambling, smoking ganja, keeping whores,
all sorts of badness and filth.[103] Tell me this now, what is a whore?
Do you think she's some form of life that wasn't made in the same
way as the rest of creation? Was it some other God who made her?
In fact, whores are just some of those women you've seduced and
lured away from their homes. Take any woman you like. Her home
can be an agony, a danger to her very life, she can be trapped, one
well in front of her and another behind, she can lose her life. But
she can't survive without someone to lean on—no matter how
brave she is, she can't stand on her own legs even in her own
house's courtyard. The reason is she's always been locked up,
strictly confined to the same house, never able to put even a foot
outside. So however bold and shameless she may be, she'd never go
chasing another man on her own. It's you that starts it off, giving
her little hints of your own bad desires, and once she's tasted them
it's enough. After that, she doesn't need a teacher to show her what
wickedness is.

It's just like when someone begins to trade in liquor or opium. They don't waste time learning what to add to the real article, what things to mix with it to make it go further, who'll sell it for them, how to keep the seller happy and get the stuff sold. Then along comes another man or woman just getting into the same line. They watch how the first one does it, learn from him and get to be experts at it themselves. It's like when any article starts selling a lot—everyone tries to manufacture it. But if there hadn't been anyone to take the initiative in the first place, no one would have started making it. It's just the same with whores. Say you'd never gone to them, never given them rupees by the hundred and your fondest respect at weddings, singing parties, receptions and other occasions and sometimes just for fun, never even given them a glance.[104] Would it be flourishing this much? In fact, it's all your fine doing. If women were terrified what would happen and how they'd manage if they ran away, they'd never put a foot outside the house. But they know very well now there's at least one way to fill their stomachs. These are the reasons it's all grown up. There's not a nest somewhere, that all prostitutes come out of. It's you who start it, speaking so sweetly to her, making her eager, luring her out over the doorstep and making her a stranger to her own house. You get along with her somehow, as long as she's in the full flush of youth; then when she's stripped and spoiled you desert her along with her fate. So she takes up the evil trade quite openly, pleasing herself and trying to get other women to join her. You can see all this from your own experience. Everyone imagines all the three worlds are made the same as themselves. To a thief's eyes everyone's a thief, to a liar everyone tells lies and to a whore everyone's depraved. And the opposite is true too: people who are charitable, pious, truthful, compassionate, guileless and forgiving— they all think the world's made like them.

When the royal sacrifice was made at the Pandavas' home in Hastanpura, Shri Krishna issued a command to Duryodhana: 'Go and choose one man out of this great gathering of rishis, a man of great virtues and qualities fit to receive a gift from my hands and bring him to me'. Duryodhana moved through all the company, but as he looked over them one by one he thought the whole lot were inferior. He went to the god and said, 'My lord, I can't find even one fit to take a gift from your hands—they're all frauds and asses'. At this, the god gave the same order to Dharmaraj. He too walked round the whole group, then the god asked, 'Well, Dharmaraj, how do you find them? Is there anyone fit to receive my gift?' Dharmaraj put his hands together and replied, 'My lord, the whole gathering shines as brightly as the sun, pure and flaming as Agni himself. How can I choose one? To my eyes, they all seem worthy of utmost reverence'.[105] It's the same in the case above.

Women are already a blazing ball of fire, so if you pour on oil will that make them burn less brightly? Get an oil-cloth torch and there's bound to be ten fireflies gathered round it![106] You get her all infatuated with you, give her all sorts of bright hopes about the future, pull her outside whichever way you can. Just ask one of these women whether this is all true, then see how she bites her lips like a tigress and grinds her teeth at your name. Wickedness just produces more wickedness, there's not an orchard where it grows somewhere. Your wickedness clings to you as thick as creepers round a vrandavan tree, but you're still very good at pushing it off on to women.[107]

Take anyone you like, man or woman, and once they've got the taste for it there's nothing wicked they won't do. You steal something and lie to cover it up, to protect that lie you have to commit even more reckless acts and on it goes. So if you hadn't eyed her invitingly in the first place none of this would have happened, would it? Now show us what women's vices come anywhere close to these. Have you seen women even once standing and staring at tamashas by the roadside, women getting drunk and lying in the road, women gambling or women swarming together in hundreds to set up as robbers? Have you ever seen them in opium shops, or openly engrossed in lovemaking in some other man's house? Prostitutes are different, so leave them out of it. It's just the way they earn their living, and if they don't do what their customers tell them, next day they go hungry.

There's a book some lucky man wrote called Stricharitra, all about wicked women.[108] But how much truth is there in all those stories? You can look as hard as you like for some real-life examples, but you won't find any. Princesses or queens—how strictly are they kept guarded and confined, then? Don't you think they might find it a bit hard to dress up in men's clothes at night and escape from the harem? Apart from the king himself, no male is ever permitted to go inside, not even a dog, and anything up to fifty hardened soldiers keep guard at the door. Are all the soldiers blind or something? Or will the darkness come down somehow and cover their eyes? You can bribe one or two of them to keep their mouths shut. But there's a whole crowd of the traitors, and surely one would raise the alarm?

In fact, how on earth would a woman have the nerve to give up her life of wealth and ease just for a gosavi or a member of the bodyguard? A woman who's never even felt the sun outside the palace, who's always been shut up, who's never seen another man's face in her life? Ah, rubbish—you'd never get that in real life.

Swans live on a diet of pearls.[109] If they had to go hungry for half the year, would they really be happy living on filth? A dancing girl just sees whoring as a way of making a living—all she cares about is the money, not who she does it with. But even a whore wouldn't set up with a palace groom or an ugly old yogi, and the same goes for a queen, however playful she is. There's quite a few stories in that Stricharitra so nasty and disgusting you feel ashamed just reading them. Anyone who reads this book will easily see what a clever patriot the author is.

Under this government, there's been a huge spread of education and printing-presses starting up. So all sorts of little books have been published—there's that one called Manjughosha, then Muktamala and the play about Manorama. Now, of course there's no pleasure in any story or book unless it has three ingredients, love, humour and grief.[110] Quite right, but an author should also think before he writes whether or not his story is true to life, whether anything like it has ever really happened, then sit down to write.

First of all then, Manjughosha, beloved daughter of an all-powerful emperor.[111] Would someone like her suddenly decide to jump into a chariot with Vasantmadhava, deceive her poor old father and run away without a thought? A father who's loved and cherished her since she was a child? Someone as clever and virtuous as her, surely she'd at least make some enquiries about this prince, who he was and where he came from, rather than just abandon her jewelled palace home and all its charming pleasures? As she was leaving, wouldn't she at least see the image of her old father before her eyes? Wouldn't she feel anything at all? So readers, you can decide for yourselves how true to life this story is. Now, thousands and thousands of years have passed since the age of the Dvaparyuga ended and the present Kaliyuga began. Even the English raj has been going now for at least two or two hundred and fifty years.[112] This author himself must have been born within this present era. So even the author's forefathers, even my fore-fathers ten generations back could never have set eyes on a heavenly chariot like Vasantmadhava's.

The English have made all sorts of machines, trains and other contraptions, even ones to send up in the sky. But even they can't make a chariot that will do whatever they want. So isn't it unlikely that Vasantmadhava could have been favoured with such a chariot and used it to run away with Manjughosha?

In the second book, Muktamala also was the high-born daughter of a chief.[113] Her husband fell out of favour with the king and got put in prison. In her struggles to see him she fell into the clutches of a wicked official called Bhadraksh. He persecuted her horribly and finished up by shutting her away in the darkness of the jungle, but she never deserted her stridharma. That's the whole story as the author tells it. All I want to say against this is, a woman's strength is like an ant against a man's. He has as much power in one hand as she has in her whole body. Imagine a tiger raging with lust and it finds a cow shut up in some quiet compound—would it really spare her life?

Even your gods are crooked, so is it any wonder that you men are villains too? Indra assumed the form of Gautama and stained the saint Ahalya's virtue.[114] Chandravali was a great pativrata, but Krishna still wrecked her vows in the guise of Rahi, didn't he?[115] Why do you cry so much about pativrata dharma, when it's you men that scheme and ruin homes and families?

Krishna's a god, and the scales that measure virtue and evil are in his hands. He's the all-seeing Atmaram, who knows all that's true and false. Women will only find release if he takes pity on them, if he destroys the lusts ingrained in you and frees women out of your clutches. Otherwise there's nothing for them. All those stories, they're only true in the book. When a brahman recites puranas, he thunders out warnings to all the listening company that egg-plants are forbidden food, never to be eaten. But when his lordship gets off his prayer-stool, those egg-plants are left where they are, in the puranas. When he gets home you'll find him smacking his lips and guzzling pounds and pounds of them.[116] So all this wisdom's just for talking, isn't it? Who follows it these days? Who cares about women's vows now? The only way she'll ever find deliverance is if she gets struck down and kills herself at the foot of the evil man, there's no other way. What's the point of writing all these stories? It's like trying to explain something to a little child. You can easily see how untrue they are compared to what usually happens. Now for the play about Manorama.[117] The author has built it round four different stories.

The first story has a happy ending because the two partners, Manorama and Ganpatrao, are both of them good-natured and well-educated. The second story shows how Godubai and Ramarao Phadnis are completely unsuited and how the young woman despised the old man and treated him with contempt. Then it describes how Godubai ran off and left him, how the magistrate went about his work, how she was disgraced before the whole court, the evidence given by the woman Saraswatibai and Tukya the barber and so on. The third story tells of Gangu, married to her inferior husband Vinayakrao. She gets lured into debauchery by Saraswatibai, runs away to Karachi and sets up openly as a whore. The story shows how much trust we should place in the kindness of a whore, her honour, her sweet words and her oaths, and describes the result of all this in the end.

In the fourth story Thaku is the widowed daughter-in-law of Rambhat the brahman. She gets pregnant, goes through all sorts of ups and downs and dies in utter misery in the Batlivala's hospital in Bombay, all this brought about through copulation.

So the author's exposed all these goings-on. But in fact he gives himself away writing a play like this, people can see through what he's up to and he just turns himself into a laughing stock. There's a saying isn't there, 'A closed fist and people think a lakh of rupees'? In fact, every house has its mud stove in it, every house has darkness in it as well as light.[118] Isn't there a sister, a mother, a daughter-in-law, a child widow in every family? If you put a stain on one of them, doesn't it stick to all of them alike? What's the use of that? Has anyone ever seen this book helping to improve every woman's fate like Manorama's, or getting all mothers and fathers to choose a fitting husband for their daughters?

It just doesn't work like that. No man's going to think to himself, 'Well, I'm old, just like Ramarao in the story, so if I marry a spirited girl like Godubai, it'll end in court with her playing games with my reputation, so I'd better not marry now I'm old'. Old men will still carry on getting married. There's no doubt it will always end in disgrace, openly or not.

Nor is it that women run away just because the man's inferior. If every woman married to a useless husband ran away today, the whole world would be full of women roaming around out of control.

As for the story about Thaku, it's no great surprise she died in hospital—someone who's going to die will die wherever they are, at home or outside. So what I want to say to you, Mr Author, is—don't even dream of pretending that the story will frighten men and women so much they'll never do it again.

So if there's an image of every wickedness it's really you men. Baba, what will you say to women then? True, there is the odd woman who does something terrible, like the old peshwa's aunt Anandibai, but that's the very rare exception.[119] When a woman like Vijaylakshmi goes wrong, every woman gets included in the blame. But the truth is you won't find ten in a hundred really like that.

And even when women do wicked things they're still better than you. First of all, you find all sorts of ways to captivate her, then once you've got her she puts complete trust in you and begins to love you right from her heart. She deserts her stridharma, the most priceless jewel she has in this world, and offers her life to you. How's she to understand your dirty tricks? At that point you make out as if you're merely her slave, you keep in her favours, you hold her shoes in your mouth to impress her, you show violent love. But how long does this love of yours last? Till your lust is satisfied. When your bad desires have been fed and there she is pregnant, you throw off all the misery and responsibility on to her and go into hiding, like a scorpion hides its face when it comes against a clod. There's the poor doe, her face like death under the burden and when she goes to ask that tiger of a man what to do, he'll answer as if he's respectability itself. 'What do you mean, what should we do? You did it, you take the consequences'. She sees that face from which she heard such tender words of love, which she gazed on like the moon, which she sacrificed herself for body and spirit, which she loved right from the soul—and now it turns on her with words like arrows in her heart. What must she feel?

But what can the poor woman do? In the end she gives up in

despair. To save her honour she even gets herself an abortion and endures all sorts of penances for her action. What has the English raj done about all this? Without witnesses, you can't do anything about it—and you can't get witnesses in such a delicate matter. But even the government is to blame for injustices here. In the case of bribes it punishes those who take bribes once and those who offer them twice. Shouldn't it pass a strict law for cases like this too, so the pair are both punished, but the woman once and the man twice? The Romans and Greeks of ancient times used to hand out very severe punishment in cases like this. So the government should turn its attention to this whole matter. If the men babble on about it, the government should just punish them further by stamping their faces with a good big stain. Then all their brothers would be so terrified we'd never have another case again. Anyway, the poor woman gets very meek and humble, she weeps for pity, she tries to wash away the stain with tears. She takes up her bundle of shame and goes off to prison or some other place, where she spends her days suffering everyone's sneers. Some women take their lives, others give up all their family and property and go into exile! Even snakes are better than you. A snake dies when you crush it, but your venom stays in the body and goes on tormenting it, and in the end it kills you. This is how you hurt people even worse than snakes. Who is it then, whose minds are so superior? Do you suffer such misery on women's behalf as they suffer for you?

Oh, we'd never find such pity and kindness at your hands. You ruin a woman one day and drive her into exile, then there you are chasing after the next. You don't even remember the first in your dreams. But a woman's love is as deep as the ocean. She'll keep to the man she loves till the end of life and beyond. He can drive her off into the jungle but she'll always take his side. Oh yes, women's hearts are filled with the tenderest love.

There are very few men who've been ruined and driven out of their homes because of a woman, but there's no saying how many women there are. You're so fiendishly clever, great thugs, very stones from the Indrayani, the blow hits home whatever we say.[120] You can walk through a field of sugar-cane and not a leaf of it touches your bodies. You hold these great meetings every day, you think up all sorts of schemes, you hold forth giving lectures, you tell other people what to do. But you yourselves, you're just clever fools. A torch shines light on other people, but right behind it everything's dark. That's how you are—if you could only see your own wickedness, your chests would burst and you'd die.

With you, you don't use the knowledge you have in your own bodies. You roam round from one place to the next, looking through all sorts of books. You get so full of learning you can play any part you please, get yourself out of difficulty—it all comes so easy to you. But these poor women, always shut in the house— what knowledge can they have, except of what's between the stove and the doorstep? And besides, women aren't just vagabonds, they're not just the bare stump of a tree like you. It's because God has weighed them down with all life's burdens that they're so easily deceived. Which of us is really soaked in wickedness, then?

Now for the eighth point—destroyers of the path to heaven, gate itself to Yama's city. Who are these women you give such names to? Whose womb did you take your birth in? Who carried the killing burden of you for nine months? Who was the saint who made you the light in her eye, who cherished you in the palm of her hand, who raised you up from a tiny scrap? Who protected and sustained you even more than her own life? Who was that then, if it wasn't your mother? And wasn't it your sister who always watched out for your welfare, who thought of you as her pride and joy, who always called you little brother so lovingly?[121] And your wife—wasn't she your companion through good times and bad, chief minister at the court of your worldly life, the one person who loved you right from the heart? These are all women too, aren't they? Or are these all different, all from a different species of women? If you talk about women, you have to talk about them all. You say women are like axes, vessels of all cunning, market-places for wickedness, wreckers of the path to heaven?

But if you hand out names like that to women, what names should we call you? Mother-haters? Slanderers of your own mothers? Even if you become a sanyasi you should still revere your mother and respect her commands. There are only three gods for children: mother, father and guru. Look at Pundalik—doing such service for his mother and father that God himself came to see, and he's still there, isn't he, standing on the same spot today? But he's seen how you honour your mothers now, so his strength has drained away—you could even go up to him and break off his foot and he still wouldn't show any of his wonderful divine power.[122] He'd just sit there silent and still. He hasn't lost the power of doing wonderful things, but he won't go near someone who's a chandal mother-hater, he won't look at his face and if he felt his touch he'd have to give himself and his clothes a purifying bath.[123] His divine qualities would be polluted if he let a chandal like that experience them. Besides, he knows the proper punishment for the wicked comes from the hands of Yamaraj—God himself seeks forgiveness there. In the story of Birbal, the emperor asked him 'Tell me now, Birbal: where exactly is God? Where does he live, what does he eat?' Birbal answered, 'Sir, God is very close to you; he lives near those who are always honest; he lives on patience and forgiveness'.[124] This means he looks on gravely and forgives the sins of the whole world. What would it be like if he didn't, if he punished every sin great and small? He'd have every minute of his time taken up trying all the hundreds of thousands of your brothers who go before him every day, sometimes a clerk, sometimes a judge, a jailer, a sepoy, an inspector, getting witnesses for them all and so on. There'd be no time to spare for his sports with the milkmaids, for his talks with Radha, Chandravali and the gopis home in Gokul![125] Well?

How would you feel if someone said about your mother, 'That old chap's mother, you know, she's a gateway to hell'. Or your sister, 'That so-and-so's sister there, she's a real storehouse of deceit'. Or your wife, 'Him over there, you know, his wife's nothing but an axe to the tree of virtue'. Would you just sit and listen to their bad words? Oh, you idiots, not even your own ancestors have ever laid eyes on heaven and you think you're going to get there? It would be good if you were shut out from heaven even if it was just one woman you'd encouraged. If it was true that all bad things you'd ever done were because of women, then all right, put the blame on their heads alone. But that's not how it is at all. You could stare at a woman's face till the day you died and it still wouldn't satisfy you, you'd die discontented, every one of you with the same fault, all alike. And what blessings you all enjoy!

Now for number nine—fitting vessels for all the sports of deceit. Aren't you just describing yourselves here? Gentlemen, you won't find anyone so full of deceit as you, not if you searched to the bottom of the earth. Women have more love for you than they do for life itself, you can't deny that. Once a woman's mind is settled in one place, it's fixed. But you men are just like bees, you like to

move on from one flower to the next. Womankind is different—
work it out for yourselves.

With one woman there, loving you with all her heart and mind,
there you are eyeing a second, then when you've had enough coming
and going with the third, off you go after number four. How can
you say that Brahma can't foretell women's lives or men's fortunes,
when your own minds are so fickle? In fact, God writes the destiny
of a man as soon as he is born, whether it's bad or good luck.
What's Brahma got to do with it? It's the potter that makes the
pots and gives them a shape. The stamp of good or evil, it's all in
Narayan's hands. Once those letters have been written on someone's forehead, not even God can change them. Who are you to
decide the truth?

The Pandavas were God's very dearest companions. Why did
they have to stay at Virata's house unrecognized, sweeping and
cleaning and so on?[126] Arjuna brought even Shankar to defeat in
battle, a man in the very mould of Indra himself. But then didn't he
take the shape of Brahannada and frolic with girls in the queen's
apartments?[127] That's what women's lives are like, but women
aren't like you, they don't give one person their hand and deal out
kicks to another. A woman will stay constant to one man, but she
needs someone whose mind matches with hers. If his won't, it
doesn't matter how much she hungers for it, thorns won't fill an
empty stomach. But you—you could be on your deathbeds and
you'd still be trying to cling on to some woman, even an ugly old
crone, like she was one of Indra's very own dancing girls—you
clever fools, you faithless, you betrayers of friends and traitors to
kings.[128] Take any name you like and you'd deserve every one of
them.

See, now, there's your friend, who's quite open and innocent
with you, and you all sweet and nice to his face. There's his lovely
companion of a wife, the breath of his life, the very Lakshmi of his
house, sword of his honour, his friend through joys and sorrows,
mistress of his wealth, sweet flower in the garden of his heart, the
fruit as tender as a pomegranate yielded him by God's favour. And
there you are—always on the look-out to see if you can snatch it
and open it up for yourself. As for a jagir or a kingdom you'll not
hesitate to pull someone down to get your hands on it. And you
still say women are fitting vessels for all sports of cunning—

congratulations, you thugs! Can you show me a single man who's been ruined for love of a woman?

Now, you'll say, haven't some great evils been caused by women? Yes, they have, all the time. Who'd say no? But what have they really done? It's you who kill each other every day over jagirs, vatans, deshmukhis, just over some little scrap of a patil's office, even poison each other.[129] Is all this women's fault too? And once it's gone to court you spend hundreds of thousands of rupees and grovel at the feet of the pettiest police constable and all for what? When you die, is it out of exhaustion or because of all your sins?

It would be quite right to blame women if they were the sole cause of evils like these. Even so, it's still the natural thing for you to offer your body for the sake of a woman—and not just the life of your body, but the whole of your life as well. The gods themselves tried to please women and make them happy, and what are you next to them? You're just leaves that fall from the trees. A woman is superior in everything, because she keeps everything under her care and all, everything, grand and splendid is for her. If there were no women you'd be wandering through the jungle eating leaves off the trees—that's what you'd feast on every day!

God made women delicate by their very nature.. So it was for them that he gave these great houses, these vadas and mansions, gardens, riches and possessions, fine garments, ease and luxury. Who cares about a vagabond like you? Neither child nor little lad. You might as well lay down your head under a tree, it makes no difference to anyone. So there's power in this half-body of woman.[130] What would you do if half your body got paralysed—could you manage on just one arm? The great power of Adimaya made all this universe.[131] She put in the body of woman a fickle strength like her own and it was her she set to drive on this cart of worldly life. You men have only one thing to do and that's fill up the cart. It's in her hands to look after it and drive it forward.[132] This is one power womankind has. Without her, you've got no greatness or grace, no triumphs, no nothing. Let's say it straight, a house without her in it seems desolate just like a burning ground. Even if it's a great palace stocked with all sorts of riches—only she can bring grace to it.

Where she makes her home, even if it's a broken-down hut held up by a couple of poles, it looks like a fine splendid temple. That's the reason people call women Lakshmi. So you think about it carefully—instead of blaming Brahma for making woman a poison like nectar and creature that binds all men in illusion, you ought to be grateful. In fact women are even more helpless than cows.[133]

For the cow to protect herself, God gave her horns sharp as spears, four legs and speed like a deer so she can escape from big savage beasts like tigers. But a woman hasn't even got these.

God didn't give these things to you either—no horns, no four legs like a horse for running away. What he gave you was just one great intelligence—he made you the greatest and best of all forms of life in the universe. So you should behave in a way that suits this high rank. But that would be hoping for too much, wouldn't it? Even that Brahma of yours who's so superior—what can we say about him, what sort of holy man has he been? He's even worse than you.

Shankar left off his penance to run after Bhil women. Vishvamitra capped it all by changing into a dog—and since then he's been making you all a bit like dogs too. There are lots of gods you could name, Chandra, Indra, and what can humans do beside these?[134]

So first of all you should bind your minds to your power of judgement that's like a strong tree-trunk and take a vow to conduct yourselves like Bhishma.[135] You should stop that maddened elephant of your lust from trampling down the plantain grove and ruining it.[136] You should start behaving with goodness and honesty; and then raise up the flag of unstained pativrata high over every house in this world, the flag that brings with it all happiness, all joyful contentment. Then look and see: doesn't even the moon look pale next to it?

But I'm not saying here that women should have freedom to do whatever their minds could want, absolutely without limits, not at all.

They may all be uneducated, ignorant and weak. But still, they should acquire strength by deciding firmly to conduct themselves properly, to be as pure as Agni inside and out, so they put men to shame and make them cast down their eyes.[137] Apart from that, their greatest ornament is to live up to their name of Lakshmi. So I pray to the great God who disposes over all, who is eternal, true and merciful, a river of compassion, a sea of forgiveness, brother of the poor. I pray women may shine like lightning by means of their conduct as pativratas in their husbands' families and their own. I pray the flag of their happiness may be raised high over the temples of both their homes, that all women and children live happily in the full glory of Lakshmi, that they should be beloved by all and their foreheads filled with the auspicious marks of marriage. I pray the lives of women in this world may at last become sweet and that all women find a place of happiness in this world and the other. So praying to God very sincerely and wishing for his welfare, I end this book.

Notes

1. Tarabai uses the term *parameshvara*, 'supreme God', here, to distinguish God as real all-powerful creator from the masculine fictions in Hindu sacred writing. She uses other terms for the same purpose more or less interchangeably: *paramatma*, *bhagavana*, *narayana*, *atmarama*.

2. The term *sahasa*, used here and in the title of the book, has a range of meanings, in some contexts, of daring and fury, audacity and violence, and in others of selfish wickedness. It is in this later sense that the term is used in nineteenth century discussions of women: see, for example, N.R. Bhagwat, *Striya sahasi kiva durachari honyas balvivah karn ahe kay?*, Bombay 1877, p. 4. Bhagwat's book, 'Does child marriage make women wicked and immoral?', defines *sahasa* as behaviour that causes harm and disgrace, and explains that women are particularly prone to it when they get into bad company or are given too much independence.

3. This is a heterogeneous list of linguistic, occupational, caste and lineage groups, the latter of elite Maratha families who led the great seventeenth century expansion of Maratha power.

4. Towns in central India famous for their handicrafts.

5. *mangalsutra:* the 'marriage-string' put round the neck of a Hindu bride at marriage and worn until she is widowed. It is one of the auspicious signs of a married woman who has her husband living. The others are the red powder *kumkum* worn as a mark on the forehead, and bangles. Tarabai refers here to the much bolder *kumkum* marks that an old-style Maratha woman would have worn, and derides the modern fashion for more delicate designs.

6. Parvati: daughter of the Himalayas and wife of the god Shiva. The reference here is probably to Paravati's feats of asceticism as she sought to win Shiva as her husband.

7. Towns in western India noted for their textile handicrafts.

8. Lakshmi: the Hindu goddess of prosperity and good fortune.

9. Tarabai uses the term *marathmola*, 'customs and practices of a real Maratha'. The most important of these is the seclusion of women. See introduction, pp.20–28.

10. *stridharma: dharma* or 'right action' for women. See introduction, pp. 29–30.

11. A reference to one of the god Krishna's boyhood pranks, a central theme in the *purana*s and other early Sanskrit texts, carried over into vernacular and oral traditions. Chandravali is the leader of the *gopi*s, the cowherd maidens whose hearts as well as their butter Krishna steals as a boy, and with whom he sports as a youth.

12. *pativrata:* the ideal wife, who devotes herself to her husband and honours him as a god. There are supposedly five great examples: Ahalya, Draupadi, Sita, Tara and Mandodari. See introduction, pp. 38–47.

13. Savitri: princess in the great epic *Mahabharata*, celebrated for her devotion to her husband: she followed him to the regions of the dead and won his soul back.

14. Another mark of ideal devotion in the *pativrata* is that she will only eat what her husband eats.

15. betet or *pan*, rolled betel leaf and areca-nut (*supari*), often flavoured with spices, sugar, lime and other ingredients, taken after eating. Tarabai hints here knowingly that the wife's refusal to share a tender after-dinner *pan* with her husband suggests also a rejection of other kinds of post-prandial intimacy.

16. *shastra*: a general term for Sanskrit digests of religious law.

17. The five Pandava brothers and their uncle Dhritarashtra, the blind king of Hastinapura, are central characters in the *Mahabharata*. Since her husband was blind, Gandhari herself always wore a bandage over her eyes. Their sons were the Kauravas, whose wars with the Pandavas form the main subject of the story.

18. *purana*: texts, usually in verse, which post-date the epics and recount the deeds of gods and goddesses; *pothi*: a general term for a book or pamphlet, often used to refer to vernacular versions of epic or puranic literature of the kind which Tarabai read. See note 25.

19. Draupadi, wife to the five Pandava brothers in the Mahabharata story. Her five husbands are explained rather apologetically: the Pandava prince Arjuna won her hand in an archery contest, and his mother Kunti told him to share whatever prize he won with his brothers, so out of deference to their mother's command Draupadi was married to all of them. She encountered Karna, son of Kunti's first marriage and bitter rival of Arjuna himself, at the contest. Karna himself later fought on the side of the Kauravas against the Pandavas on the battlefield of Kurukshetra.

20. Ahalya appears in the epic *Ramayana* as the beautiful wife of the sage Gautama, guru to the god Indra. Gautama caught Indra making love to his wife and cursed her so she turned to stone. In some versions Ahalya knows Indra and is flattered; in others Indra only gets his way by disguising himself as Gautama. Ahalya was eventually redeemed by Rama and restored to her husband, to become a great *pativrata*.

21. Satyavati, nymph, fishermaid and mother of some of the main characters in the *Mahabharata*. The sage Parashara saw her playing in a stream and told her she would give birth to a prodigy if they made love. She was half-willing, but embarrassed because she smelled of fish. He convinced her by changing her smell into fragrance. From the union she bore Vyasa, author of the Vedas, then went on to marry a king, Shantanu. Their two sons died childless, so Satyavati instructed Vyasa to provide the widows with sons. The sons so born were Dhritarashtra and Pandu, fathers of the Kauravas and Pandavas respectively. Kunti was a princess who so devoted herself to the sage Durvasa that he gave her a *mantra* or magic charm by which she could call gods and make them do her bidding. She called up Surya, the sun, and by him bore Karna, but had to give him away as she was unmarried. She went on to marry Pandu and bear the Pandavas.

22. love marriage: *gandharva vivaha* is classified in Manu as one of the eight legitimate forms of marriage: see G. Buhler (ed.), *The Laws of Manu*, Delhi 1979, p. 81. It is so called because of the free love supposed to exist among these celestial beings.

23. Vidur: son of a union between Vyasa and a slave girl.

24. The story of Rama, incarnation of Vishnu and eldest son of Dasaratha, king of Ayodhya, forms the main theme of the *Ramayana*. Dasaratha banished his son at the instigation of one of his wives, Kaikeyi, who wished her own son Bharata on the throne. Rama's brother Lakshman and his faithful wife Sita accompanied

him. During their exile the demon king Ravana abducted Sita, and she was eventually rescued from Lanka by Rama in alliance with Sugriva, king of the monkeys. Sugriva himself had been driven from his throne by his usurping half-brother, Vali. Rama helped Sugriva recover his kingdom and his wife, and after Vali's death arranged for his widow, Tara, to marry Sugriva himself.

25. Shridhar, a brahman of Pandharpur writing in the mid-sixteenth century, author of the *Ramavijaya* and *Pandavapratapa*, Marathi versions of the *Ramayana* and *Mahabharata* respectively. These found a much wider and more popular audience than the Sanskrit originals, and their public or private reading was one means through which the unlearned had access to the epics. Editions were published in 1876 and 1868 respectively, but neither of the texts has ever been stabilized in a standard critical edition. Tarabai was familiar with both, and in many of her detailed references to episodes from the epics, used these Marathi versions rather than the Sanskrit originals. See introduction, pp. 42–3.

26. Ravana's austerities led the gods to give him the boon of invincibility in battle, but a curse was laid on him that he would die through a woman's doing.

27. Ravana's wife Mandodari is celebrated in the *Ramayana* as a great *pativrata*. She warned him against seizing unwilling women and tried without success to get him to send Sita back. Tarabai follows Shridhar's Marathi version very closely here: see *Ramavijaya*, 24, 80–116. For these themes in twentieth-century women's folk-songs, see I. Junghare and J. Frater, 'The Ramayana in Maharashtrian Women's Folk-Songs', *Man In India*, vol. 56, 1976, p. 295.

28. Angada was the son of Vali the monkey king and his wife Tara. This episode does not appear in the published *Ramavijaya* that I have seen, and may likewise come from a different text or from oral versions of the story.

29. Indrajit was Ravana's son, slain when Lakshman cut his head off. His faithful wife Sulochana came to the enemy camp to ask for her husband's head back. Impressed by her devotion, Rama was about to bring Indrajit back to life. He was persuaded not to by the monkey army, who wished to see Bibhishan, estranged brother of Ravana and ally of Rama, placed on the throne of Lanka. Sulochana went as *sati* on Indrajit's pyre. This is Shridhar almost word for word: see *Ramavijaya*, 30, 174–6.

30. *rishi*: a sage, of whom many appear in the epics and *purana*s, with a range of different stories about their parentage.

31. Bhagiratha: a son of the kings of Ayodhya, who laboured to bring the sacred river Ganges down from the celestial regions to earth. Jaimini: a disciple of Vyasa, and a celebrated sage.

32. Literally, 'not one of you picks up the hero's vida'. *Vida* is a roll of betel leaves. The phrase 'to pick up the vida' means to accept a challenge, and originates in the Maratha practice 'of throwing a *vida* into the midst of an assembly (as of warriors, statesmen, etc.) in indication of defiance or invitation to some arduous work': see Molesworth, *A Dictionary of Marathi and English*, p. 757.

33. *sanyasi*: one who has abandoned all worldly ties, the last of the four ideal stages in the life of a high-caste Hindu man. This first three are *brahmachari*, *grhastha* and *vanaprastha*: celibate student, householder and forest-dweller. Tarabai's language here recalls the common metaphor of woman as the field in which man sows his seed. See Wadley, 'Women in the Hindu Tradition', in R. Ghadially (ed.), *Women in Indian Society*, pp. 26–7.

34. *darshan:* 'taking sight' of a god or shrine, which confers blessing in itself. Agastya: a celebrated sage who befriended Rama during his exile.

35. Tarabai uses the term *shakti* to describe this special power of women. See introduction, pp. 54–5.

36. The power of women's eyes, piercing like arrows into the hearts of men, is a common motif at many cultural levels in South Asia—but employed here to make rather a different kind of point about the power of women.

37. Tarabai echoes an absolutely central theme in women's oral culture here, where a mother's love, its innocence, its constancy, its sweet selfless depths, forms a very strong value in women's songs, often accompanied by bitter reproaches for those who hold mothers cheap. See A. Bhagwat, 'Maharashtrian Folk-Songs on the Grind-Mill', *Journal of the University of Bombay*, January 1942, pp. 138–62, and Mary Fuller, 'Marathi Grinding Songs', *New Review*, June 1940, p. 512.

38. i.e., 'Might is right', 'Possession is nine-tenths of the law'.

39. rights: I have translated the term *sikka* as 'rights', but it has a range of meanings rather different from its western sense. *Sikka* refers to a seal or stamp in general, but more specifically the royal signet or seal placed upon any grant of rights in pre-colonial Maharashtra.

40. Yama: the god of the dead, whose messengers summon the living and who sits in judgement on their souls in his city in the lower world.

41. A common phrase for someone that no one looks after or cares about: see Date and Karve, *Maharashtra vakya-samparadaya kosha*, vol. i, p. 145.

42. Ten days is the standard period of Hindu mourning for close relatives, during which no marriage or other auspicious ceremony is held.

43. Rani of Jhansi: Lakshmibai was queen of the small Maratha state of Jhansi, annexed in 1854 under Dalhousie's doctrine of lapse (see note 79). She fought on the rebel side during the rebellion of 1857 and was killed in the seige of Gwalior in 1858. Her name became a byword for women's daring and courage.

44. *battislakshani:* the thirty-two marks of excellence—i.e., someone so superior that they have them all. They refer to the proper proportions and colours of different parts of the body. See Date and Karve, *Maharashtra vakya-sampradaya kosha*, vol ii, p. 258. The term lends itself best to sarcasm, as is the case here.

45. Men's lack of affection compared to the devotion of wives and mothers is another theme in women's songs: see Mary Fuller, 'Maher', *Man in India*, vol. 22, 1942, p. 118; Bhagwat, 'Maharashtrian Folk-Songs', p. 171.

46. *sandice khapara*, 'pot in the corner', a rich Marathi reference to a widow. The widow is a pot or vessel, a common symbol for the female, but she is no longer used by the family and so thrown aside into the corner. Anything which is 'in the corner' also has the implication of something improper, fit only for a secret place, reflecting the association of widows with illicit sex and prostitution.

47. i.e., the punishment for a crime visited on a party quite innocent.

48. *math:* a monastery, community of Hindu ascetics and scholars.

49. i.e., superior goods will always be valued over inferior, no matter what condition they are in.

50. This proverb means that a wife's attention is worth most in times of real sickness or adversity.

51. i.e., if you're a man, you can always get some form of honour—*amir, fakir* and *pir* translate as lord, mendicant and saint respectively. A pointed proverb to the effect that men demand respect no matter what their rank or stage of life.

52. See note 33.

53. The joke here is that the ritual of a man's becoming *sanyasi* should really begin with a sacrificial fire at sunset.

54. For Vijaylakshmi's crime and trial, see introduction, p. 1.

55. *panchagavya* penance: a powerful rite of purification in which the offender consumes the five products of the cow (milk, curds, ghee, dung and urine). For liberals and reformers who had broken caste rules by travelling abroad, eating the wrong food or associating with the widow-remarriage movement, this was a common means of purifying themselves. See introduction, p. 14.

56. This proverb reflects the intense loyalty and protectiveness women are supposed to feel to their own homes and families, and equally intense reticence and suspicion towards outsiders.

57. Manu: Tarabai plays on the double meaning of this term. Manu is the author of the Institutes of Manu, most authoritative of orthodox Hindu law-books, but the name is also generic: each age has its Manu, and the passing of ages is measured by each one. Thus Manu also has the meaning of time, age or season, reflected in the emphasis here on the changes time has brought.

58. *vada:* a substantial but old-fashioned style of house, built on several floors around a courtyard, and probably much better suited to the fluctuating needs of a joint family than the less flexible accomodation of a modern single-storey bungalow.

59. Maratha men in mourning at this time did not wear a proper turban, but tied a *dhoti* or loincloth round their heads. From this remark Telugu men also seem to have been notorious for their untidy turbans.

60. *dvaparayuga:* there are four *yuga*s or ages in the elaborate cycles of creation and decay described by Hindu cosmology. These are the *satya, treta, dvapara* and *kali*. After the perfection of the first, each marks a further stage in the world's degeneration, until Vishnu returns to destroy it and enable the cycle to begin again.

61. A great chariot was one of Indrajit's weapons in the *Ramayana*.

62. *bavanakhani:* the old red-light district of Poona city.

63. To give or let water go is a Marathi way of describing an act of giving which is final and irreversible, just as the gift of a girl to her husband is irreversible. In Maratha marriage ceremonies in the nineteenth century, one or both parents of the bride poured water over the groom's hands: T. Broughton, *Letters from a Mahratta Camp*, London, 1892, p. 140.

64. Tarabai echoes another theme strong not only in women's oral tradition, but in regional culture more widely. This is a girl's intense happiness at her *maher*, her maternal home, where she is especially cherished as a little girl because her parents know she must leave them, and to which she returns with relief and delight after her travails as a daughter-in-law at her husband's home. See Fuller, 'Maher', pp. 116–22.

65. The hardships of a young daughter-in-law are, of course, another pervasive theme in women's songs: her backbreaking work, her anxiety to please, her dependence and juniority, the scoldings she suffers mutely: see Fuller, 'Maher', pp. 114–17; Junghare and Frater, 'The Ramayana', pp. 301–3; Bhagwat, 'Maharashtrian Folk-Songs', p. 171.

66. Here Tarabai starts to address the gods in the familiar Marathi form *tu*, the better to express her anger and contempt.

67. A woman's toiling in her husband's house like a hired bullock is a common image in women's songs: a hired bullock, of course, is one that you get as much work out of as you can. See Fuller, 'Maher', p. 117; Bhagwat, 'Maharashtrian Folk-Songs', p. 171.

68. a pinch of grain: figurative expression for a woman's personal property, that portion of the household's resources which she can call her own. cf., the Tamil 'a handful of rice', to mean a woman's personal property.

69. Vidhatya is a name of Brahma as he ordains and arranges fates. A very common image in regional culture is of his writing the destiny of every individual on the forehead at birth: Bhagwat, 'Maharashtrian Folk-Songs', July 1941, p. 151. The curses here refer, of course, to women's cursing of their luck for having been born as women.

70. This refers to Dasaratha's bitter reflections in the *Ramayana* on the cupidinious nature of women, after Kaikeyi tricks him into promising to exile Rama. Tarabai later quotes from the rendering of this passage in Shridhar's *Ramavijaya*. See note 73.

71. These are characters in epic and *puranic* stories celebrated for their fortitude.

72. I think what Tarabai means here is that unlike women, rulers and children have in their different ways always been able to make demands, to be obstinate, to get their own way.

73. Tarabai quotes fragments from one of the printed versions of Shridhar's *Ramavijaya*, where Dasaratha reproaches Kaikeyi for her treachery and greed. See *Ramavijaya* 1876, 9, 188–91.

74. Tarabai quotes in its original Sanskrit from the *sataka-trayam*, 'Three centuries of verse' of the poet Bharatṛhari. However, her source for this verse was not the Sanskrit original, but one of the early Marathi romantic novels that she attacks later in her text (see note 105). This is Naro Sadasiv Risbud's *Manjughosa*. Risbud gives not only the Sanskrit but also a Marathi translation, which runs as follows:

    That device of woman has a force stronger even than evil incantations. Whirled about by many whims; the very abode of debauchery; a very city of thoughtlessness; storehouse of all guilt; soaked a hundred times over in deceit; the beginning of all wickedness; destroyers of the path to heaven; the gate itself to Yama's city; fitting vessel for all sports of deceit; this is the nature of woman, a poison seeming like nectar; thus Brahmadeva has created this device of woman, cord that snares creatures in the world of illusion.

    N.R. Risbud, *Manjugosha*, Poona 1875, p. 66. The language of Tarabai's subsequent commentary makes it clear that it is Risbud's Marathi she is using, rather than the Sanskrit.

75. From here onwards, Tarabai takes Risbud's Marathi to pieces and refutes each of its criticisms in a series of points, which she numbers from one to nine.

76. *avichara* translates literally as 'thoughtless', but means much more than that; it means light-minded, irresponsible, indiscreet, heedless or incapable of proper forms of conduct and restraint—one of the characteristic defects of women from the point of view of someone like Shridhar, writing within the brahmanical tradition.

77. Meru: the great mountain that stands at the centre of the world in Hindu mythical geography, used here as a metaphor.

78. Another strong theme in women's songs is the joy that her husband brings a woman. Her *kumkum*, *mangalsutra* and bangles, auspicious signs of her wifehood, are more precious than any worldly riches; but conversely, for a woman without a husband the world can only be a desolate wilderness. See Fuller, 'Maher', pp. 119–21; Bhagwat, 'Maharashtrian Folk-Songs', January 1942, pp. 137–140.

79. Here, Tarabai refers to the doctrine of lapse employed during the Marquess of Dalhousie's term as Governor-General of India (1848–56), by which the states of Hindu princes without direct heirs were annexed. The case of the Maratha state of Nagpur in 1854 aroused particular public attention for the way that the women of the palace were treated.

80. Complaints against fathers for the marriages they arrange form another stock theme in women's song: fathers who sell their daughters to old men for money, who give them to men who beat and harass them, or who marry them to men who have wives already, with all the pains and jealousies attendant on that position. Here, Tarabai articulates what seems to be an almost stock list of women's complaints. See Fuller, 'Marathi Grinding Songs', p. 515; Bhagwat, 'Maharashtrian Folk-Songs', July 1941, pp. 159–61.

81. *sati:* a widow's immolation on her husband's funeral pyre, the ultimate expression of her devotion as *pativrata*.

82. Sarvajanik Sabha: a proto-nationalist public association founded in Poona in 1870, whose members set themselves up as mediators between government and people in the presidency. It published its proceedings in its *Quarterly Journal*, launched in 1878.

83. cow-dung cakes: when dried, these are a common form of fuel.

84. The comparison of women with cows is a common motif in regional culture: both are meek and helpless, both subject to others' authority, both must stay where their owners tie them, both must bear their trials dumbly. Women's songs liken giving a girl to a bad husband to selling a cow to the butcher. See Fuller, 'Marathi Grinding Songs', p. 515.

85. The proverb implies the painful dilemma of someone whose every option is closed to them.

86. Pigs cleaning up excrement would have been and still are a common sight in rural and small-town India. Here, of course, Tarabai intends the image to convey how women go to the bad in their husbands' absence.

87. Here, Tarabai may have had a specific case in mind: see introduction, p. 59.

88. This is probably a reference to the Bengali reformer Vidyasagara, whose name translates also as 'ocean of wisdom'. He attempted to encourage the remarriage of widows by using his own income to give men financial incentives, and was ruined and disillusioned in the process. See introduction, p. 13.

89. This was something like Tarabai's own position; see introduction, pp. 5–6.

90. Appasahib and Babasahib: terms of respect. Men's passion for new wives and neglect of the old is a common women's theme: see Bhagwat, 'Maharashtrian Folk-Songs', January 1942, pp. 142–3.

91. These are types of ascetics in contemporary popular religion.

92. Radha is the beautiful milkmaid and consort of the god Krishna.

93. *dama* is money; it is 'Mr Money' that the holy man meditates on so profoundly.

94. Sambha: a name of Shiva.
95. Kashi: the sacred city of Banaras. Viththal is one of Maharashtra's most popular deities, assumed to be an incarnation of Krishna. His image stands on a brick in his shrine at the sacred city of Pandharpur. The god came to Pandharpur to show his delight at the filial devotion of Pundalik, one of the brahmans of the city.
96. Sri Bhagirathi: the Ganges, from the god who brought the river to earth. See note 31.
97. Tarabai's fake holy man repeats names of Visnu here: 'great god, he who rests on the serpent Shesa, oh Shrinarayana...'. His *gomukhi* (lit. 'cow mouth') is a glove shaped like a cow's mouth, worn whilst telling the sacred *tulasi* beads.
98. Subhadra is Krishna's sister, born into the celebrated Yadava lineage. At Krishna's suggestion, Arjuna carried her off and she became his wife. Tarabai quotes here almost verbatim from one of the printed versions of Sridhar: see *Pandavapratap* 1868, 13, 215–6.
99. It is Vishnu who is invoked here; he reclines on the serpent Shesa at the bottom of Kshirasagar, the sea of milk.
100. A reference to the last episodes of the *Ramayana*. Rama refused to take Sita back after her rescue from Lanka, unable to believe she had remained faithful during her years in captivity. An ordeal by fire proved her innocence, but Rama's subjects in Ayodhya still whispered against her, so Rama sent her away to a hermitage.
101. Here, Tarabai lists the cures for female barrenness used by her female contemporaries, such as eating the umbilical cord from a new baby or visiting temples of the bachelor god Maruti (Hanuman) naked on a new moon night. See *Central Provinces District Gazetteers, Buldhana District*, p. 158.
102. The image of lovers as bees feeding on honey and nectar is a very common one in Sanskrit and vernacular love poetry.
103. *tamasha*: a popular form of village entertainment, with sketches, dances, singing and so on. Boys usually played women characters.
104. Courtesans and dancing girls were invited to perform at weddings and other celebrations of the well-to-do, and favoured with gifts for their skills at singing and dancing.
105. Duryodhana is the jealous and ambitious leader of the Kaurava brothers, who led them into battle against the Pandavas. Dharmaraja is another name of Yama, god of death and justice. Here again, Tarabai follows Shridhar's Marathi very closely: see *Pandavapratap*, 17, 177–86.
106. *divata*, a firefly, also has the meaning of a rogue, a man who causes shame or disgrace. Just as fireflies collect round a big torch, so rogues gather round a woman.
107. *vrandavan*: a Colocynth tree, which has creepers clustered thickly round it.
108. *Stricharitra:* 'Portrait of Woman'. See introduction, pp. 40–42.
109. Swans are a common image for lovers in Sanskrit and vernacular love poetry, and depicted as living on pearls.
110. Here, Tarabai repeats the formula for a successful story given in one of the *Stricharitra:* see *Vidagdha Stri Charitra*, by Chintaman Dixit Joshi, Satara 1871, p. 49.
111. See introduction, pp.42–3.
112. An exaggeration, of course; the establishment of East Indian Company 'rule' (*raj*) in India was a gradual process, but did not really begin as a political process until the 1750s in Bengal.

113. See introduction, pp. 45–6.
114. See note 20.
115. See note 11.
116. 'Letting the egg-plant stay in the *puranas*': a proverb for people who do not practise as they preach.
117. See introduction, pp. 43–4.
118. i.e., discretion or concealment is the best way of winning respect; if you've only got something cheap or mean to show, better to keep it covered up. A *chula*, mud stove, is a universal kitchen item in India wherever wood is used as a fuel. The sense here is that every house has various categories of women in it, just as every one has a *chula*, so none can claim special purity or superiority.
119. Anandibai was the wife of Raghunathrao, ambitious uncle of the young Maratha ruler Narayanarao peshwa in the 1770s. Narayanarao was murdered in August 1773 and succeeded by Raghunathrao; Anandibai was suspected by many contemporaries of having taken part in the murder.
120. The Indrayani is the holy river at Dehu near Poona, into which the books of the Marathi poet-saint Tukaram were thrown by the local brahmans. The river returned the books to him. 'Stones of Indrayani' may therefore be a sarcastic way of referring to men's presumed holiness.
121. A sister's love, especially for a younger brother, is also an important value in women's songs: see Bhagwat, 'Maharashtrian Folk-songs', July 1941, pp. 163–85.
122. Tarabai refers to the image of Vithoba at Pandharpur here (see note 95). She may have had in mind an incident in 1873, when Vithoba's feet were broken off by two overenthusiastic *gosavi* mendicants: see *Sholapur Gazetteer*, pp. 423.
123. *chandal:* a term of extreme revilement—a filthy, loathsome, wicked pariah of a person.
124. Birbal: the famous brahman minister and counsellor to the sixteenth century Mughal emperor Akbar.
125. Gokul: the pastoral regions where Krishna spent his boyhood with the cowherds.
126. An episode from the *Mahabharata*: having lost their kingdom in a game of dice, the Pandavas spent the last year of their exile disguised as brahmans, in the service of Virata, king of the Matsyas.
127. Arjuna, third Pandava brother and son of Indra, disguised himself as the eunuch Brahannada while the brothers were at Virata's court. He was employed to teach music and dancing to the princesses at court.
128. In epics and *purana*s much is made of Indra's fondness for women, as in the story of Ahalya (see note 20). Indra's heaven comes with its own beautiful courtesans.
129. These are names of offices and categories of title to land.
130. *ardhanga*, lit. 'half-body', a common term for a wife, who is the half-body of her husband.
131. Adimaya: the primal mother. For Tarabai's use of these very positive images of woman, see introduction, pp. 54–6.
132. 'a fickle strength'. The term *chanchalata* means fickle, capricious, fleeting, unstable or wanton, especially when applied to a woman. Here again, Tarabai takes one of the negative qualities that orthodox Hinduism ascribed to women, and claims it as a virtue.
133. See note 84.

134. These are references to the misdemeanours of these figures from the epics and *puranas*. Shankar is a name of Shiva, one of whose characteristics is his power of asceticism. The Bhils are a tribal group in western India. The sage Vishvamitra appears at one point in the *Mahabharata* eating the flesh of a dog during a famine, which may have given rise to stories of his changing into a dog. Chandra is Soma, the moon in puranic mythology. He stole the sage Brihaspati's wife, which brought him into conflict with Indra, Brihaspati and the gods.

135. Bhishma: son of Shantanu and the river goddess Ganga. He helped arrange the union that produced the half-brothers Dhritarashtra and Pandu (see note 21). In the war between Kauravas and Pandavas he sided with the former and died at the hands of Arjuna, but his fidelity, moderation and self-denial won him great admiration.

136. plantain-grove: a female plaintain tree often stands in women's songs for a chaste woman, and its fruit or flowers for her children. The image comes from the idea that a female banana tree is very chaste because she obtains her fruits without any male member. See Bhagwat, 'Maharashtrian Folk-Songs', July 1941, p. 143.

137. i.e., a reversal of the more usual model for womanly modesty.

Glossary

amir	a lord, nobleman
bairagi	a mendicant devoted to the god Vishnu
bavankhani	the old 'red light' district of Poona city
battislakshani	one who has the 'thirty-two marks of excellence' set out in treatises on palmistry
bhadramahila	a woman of the Bengali *bhadralok*, or upper classes
bhakti	the long-standing devotional tradition in western India's popular religious culture
bharati	a mendicant who recites the epic *Mahabharata*
Bhatia	a merchant caste from Gujarat
Bhil	a tribal community in north Maharashtra and Gujarat
brahmachari	a celibate student, the first of the four ideal stages in the life of an orthodox Hindu. The others are householder, forest-dweller and renouncer
burqa	the all-enveloping outer garment worn by women in purdah outside the home
buva	respectful term for a mendicant, guru or senior person generally
chandal	term of revilement for an untouchable
darshan	the 'sight' of a god or other high personage, conferring merit and blessing
desai	the hereditary landlord and revenue collector of a district
deshmukh	another term for a hereditary landlord and revenue collector
dharma	the proper moral order of things
dhoti	a loincloth, often worn elaborately folded
Dubla	a low caste labouring community of Gujarat
dudhahari	an ascetic who lives only on milk
Dvaparyuga	the third of the four *yuga*s or ages of Hindu mythology
fakir	general term for a Muslim mendicant
gharjavai	a son-in-law who comes to live at his wife's natal home
ghat	steps or landing-place on a river or tank
ghosha	Marathi term for female seclusion
Gingar	a caste of small traders, specializing in wood and leather
giripuri	a religious mendicant who whirls around continuously
gomukhi	glove shaped like the mouth of a cow, worn while telling the beads of a rosary
gopi	milkmaid, especially those depicted in the epics sporting with the young Krishna
gosavi	general term for a religious ascetic, usually lower-caste

haridasi	a mendicant who recites stories of the god Vishnu
inam	a tenure of land exempt from taxation
inamdar	holder of an *inam*
jaggery	coarse brown sugar made from palm sap
jagir	an assignment of land or land-revenue
jagirdar	holder of a *jagir*
jatadhari	a mendicant with long and matted hair
jogi	general term for a mendicant or ascetic
joshi	general term for a priest
kanbi	Gujarati term for a farmer or cultivator
Khatri	a caste of silk-weavers
kshatriya	a warrior, one of the four ranks or *varna*s of the Hindu tradition
kanphota	a mendicant with heavily pierced ears
Kasar	a caste of metal workers
Komti	a well-to-do caste of small traders, metalworkers and artisans
kumkum	red powder worn as an auspicious mark on the forehead of a Hindu wife to indicate that her husband is living
kunbi	a farmer or cultivator within the larger Maratha caste complex
lakh	a hundred thousand
maher	a woman's natal home
Mali	a caste of gardeners
mamledar	an official or revenue collector for a district
mangalsutra	the 'marriage-string' put round the neck of a Hindu bride at marriage and worn until she is widowed
mantra	a mystical verse or incantation
Manu	the great lawgiver of the Hindu tradition; also a term for an age or time
Maratha	the dominant warrior-peasant caste of western India
marathmola	'Maratha custom', meaning the seclusion of women in particular
Marwadi	a merchant and moneylending caste from Marwad in Rajasthan
math	a monastery or community of ascetics and scholars
munsif	a low-ranking native judge
nanakpanthi	a follower of Nanak, founder of the Sikh religious community
nange	a naked mendicant
ovi	a Marathi verse form
padar	the end of a woman's sari, which can be drawn over the head for modesty
pan	betel nut and other ingredients, rolled in a leaf for chewing
panchagavya	a form of penance, involving consumption of the five products of the cow: curds, ghee, urine, dung, milk
pat	the second marriage of a woman

Patidar	a dominant farming caste in Gujarat
patil	headman of a village
pativrata	the ideal wife, who devotes herself utterly to her husband
pir	a Muslim saint
pothi	general term for a book or pamphlet
Prabhu	a caste of writers
purana	sacred Hindu texts, supposedly 18 in number, recounting the deeds of the gods
ramgiribuva	mendicant devoted to the worship of Rama
Rajput	a warrior and landholding caste in Rajputana
rishi	a sage or seer
sadhu	general term for an ascetic or holy man
sanyasi	a renouncer, last in the four ideal stages in the life of a Hindu man.
sati	the ritual immolation of a widow with her husband's body
shastra	general term for Sanskrit digests of Hindu religious law
shastribuva	one who is versed in the *shastra*s
Shenvi	a lesser caste of brahmans
sloka	a verse of two lines
stridharma	*dharma* or right action for women
shudra	the lowest of the four ranks or *varna*s of Hindu tradition
tamasha	a popular musical performance, often with ribald content
tulsi	a kind of basil, sacred to many Hindus
vada	an old-style great house or mansion, built around a courtyard
vakil	an attorney; barrister; pleader
zenana	the quarters of a house reserved for women in purdah

Bibliography

Records and Official Publications

Central Provinces District Gazetteers
Director of Ethnography for India, MSS. Eur. D. 356, Oriental and India Office Collections.
Gazetteers of the Bombay Presidency
Imperial Census of 1881: Operations and Results in the Presidency of Bombay, Government Central Press, 1882.
Reports on Native Newspapers for the Bombay Presidency
Selections from the Records of the Government of India in the Home Department, No. CCXXIII: Papers relating to Infant Marriage and Enforced Widowhood. Government Printing Press, Calcutta 1886.

Newspapers

Dnyanodaya
Kesari
Grihini
Indian Spectator
Indu Prakash
Times of India
Vichardarpan

Books and articles

Banerjee, S. 'Marginalisation of Women's Popular Culture in Nineteenth Century Bengal', in K. Sangari and S. Vaid (eds.) *Recasting Women: Essays in Colonial History*, Kali for Women, New Delhi 1989.

Bapat, R. 'Pandita Ramabai', mimeo, 1990.

Bayly, C. 'From Ritual to Ceremony: Death ritual in Hindu North India since 1600', in J. Whaley (ed.) *Mirrors of Mortality: Studies in the Social History of Death*, Europa, London, 1981.

——, *Rulers, Townsmen and Bazaars: North Indian Society in the Age of British Expansion*, Cambridge University Press, 1983.

——, *Indian Society and the Making of the British Empire*, Cambridge University Press, 1988.

Bayly, S. *Saints, Goddesses and Kings: Muslims and Christians in South Indian Society 1700–1900*, Cambridge University Press, 1990.

Bhagwat, A. 'Maharashtrian Folk Songs on the Grind-Mill', *Journal of the University of Bombay*, July 1941 & January 1942.

Bhagwat, N. *Striya sahasi kiva durachari honyas balvivah karn ahe kay?* Bombay, 1877.

Birze, V. *Kshatriya va tyance astitva*, Baroda, 1903.

Borthwick, M. *The Changing Role of Women in Bengal, 1849–1905*, Princeton University Press, 1984.

Breman, J. *Of Peasants, Migrants and Paupers: Rural Labour Circulation and Capitalist Production in West India*, Oxford University Press, Delhi 1985.

Broughton, T. *Letters from a Mahratta Camp during the Year 1809*, London 1892.

Buhler, G. (ed.) *The Laws of Manu*, Delhi 1979.

Carroll, L. 'Colonial Perceptions of Indian Society and the Emergence of Caste(s) Associations', *Journal of Asian Studies*, XXXVII, 2, 1978.
'Law, custom and statutory social reform: the Hindu Widows' Remarriage Act of 1856', *Indian Economic and Social History Review*, 20, 4, 1983.

Chakravarti, U. 'Whatever happened to the Vedic Dasi?' in K. Sangari and S. Vaid (eds.) *Recasting Women: Essays in Colonial History*, Kali for Women, New Delhi, 1989.

Chandra, S. 'Social background to the rise of the Maratha movement during the 17th. century in India', *Indian Economic and Social History Review*, September 1983.

Chatterjee, P. 'The Nationalist Resolution of the Woman's Question' in K. Sangari and S. Vaid (eds.) *Recasting Women: Essays in Colonial History*, Kali for Women, New Delhi 1989.

Chavan, V. *Bhandari Lokanca Vrattant*, Bombay, 1887.

Chintamani, C. (ed.) *Indian Social Reform*, Madras, 1901.

Chitale, M. *Manorama Nataka*, Bombay, 1871.

Choksey, R. *Mountstuart Elphinstone: The Indian Years*, Bombay 1871.

Chowdhry, P. 'Custom in a Peasant Economy: Women in colonial Haryana' in K. Sangari and S. Vaid (eds.) *Recasting Women: Essays in Colonial History*, Kali for Women, New Delhi 1989.

Clark, A. 'Limitations on female life chances in rural central Gujarat' in J. Krishnamurty, (ed.) *Women in Colonial India: Survival, Work and the State*, Oxford University Press, Delhi 1989.

Clark, T. (ed.) *The Novel in India: Its Birth and Development,* London, 1970.

Coats, T. 'Account of the Present State of the Township of Lony', *Transactions of the Literary Society of Bombay*, vol. iii, 1823.

Dasgupta, S and R. Hedge, 'The Eternal Receptacle: a Study of Mistreatment of Women in Hindi Film' in R. Ghadially (ed.) *Women in Indian Society*, New Delhi 1988.

Date, Y. and C. Karve, *Maharashtra Shabda-kosha*, Poona 1932–8.

Desai, S. *Social Life in Maharashtra under the Peshwas*, Bombay 1980.
A Dictionary of the Maratha Language, Compiled by Jugunnauth Shastree Kramuvunt and others in the service of the Bombay Education Society, Bombay 1829.

Dirks, N. 'The invention of caste: civil society in colonial India, *Social Analysis*, 25, September 1989.

Feldhaus, A. 'Bahina Bai: Wife and Saint', *Journal of the American Academy of Religion*, 1982.

Forbes, J. *Oriental Memoirs,* London 1813.

Fox-Genovese, E. 'Culture and consciousness in the intellectual history of European women', *Signs*, 12, 3, 1987.

Fukazawa, H. 'State and caste system (jati) in the eighteenth century Maratha kingdom', *Hitotsubashi Journal of Economics*, 9, 1, June 1968.

Fuller, M. 'Marathi Grinding Songs', *New Review*, June 1940.

——, 'Maher', *Man in India*, 22, 1942.

Ghadially, R. *Women in Indian Society*, New Delhi, 1988.

Gokhale, B. *Poona in the eighteenth Century: An Urban History*, Oxford University Press, Delhi, 1988.

Gordon, S. (ed.) *Kingship and Authority in South Asia*, University of Wisconsin-Madison Press, 1981.

Gunnojee, R. *Stree Churitra or Female Narration*, Bombay, 1882.

Halbe, L. *Muktamala*, Bombay, 1851.

Hardy, F. (ed.) 'The Diary of an Unknown Indian Girl', *Religion*, 1980.

Hawley, J and D. Wulf (eds.) *The Divine Consort: Radha and the Goddesses of India*, University of California Press, Berkeley, 1982.

Haynes, D. and P. Prakash, (eds.) *Contesting Power: Resistance and Everyday Social Relations in South Asia*, Oxford University Press, Delhi, 1991.

Jacobson, D. 'The chaste wife: cultural norm and individual experience' in S. Vatuk (ed.) *American Studies in the Anthropology of India*, New Delhi 1978.

Jambhekar, G. (ed.) *Memoirs and Writings of Acharya Bal Shastri Jambhekar*, Bombay 1950.

Jeffery, P. *Frogs in a Well: Indian Women in Purdah*, London, 1979.

Jenkins, R. *Report on the Territories of the Rajah of Nagpore submitted to the Supreme Government of India*, Calcutta, 1827.

Joglekar, D. *Independent Widows and their Youthful Daughters*, Bombay, 1888.

Johnson, G. *Provincial Politics and Indian Nationalism: Bombay and the Indian National Congress 1885–1915*, Cambridge University Press, 1973.

Jones, K. *Socio-Religious Reform Movements in British India*, Cambridge University Press, 1989.

Joshi, N. *Punevarnana*, Bombay 1868.

Joshi, C. *Vidagdha Stri Charitra*, Satara 1871.

Junghare, I and J. Frater, 'The Ramayana in Maharashtrian Women's Folk-Songs', *Man in India*, 56, 1976.

Kadam, V. 'The institution of marriage and position of women in eighteenth century Maharashtra', *Indian Economic and Social History Review*, 25, 3, 1988.

Kanitkar, G. *Sushikshita Stricharitra*, Bombay, 1872.

Khalatkar, N. *Marathance rudhi ani sudharana*, Nagpur, 1907.

Khan, M. 'Vindication of the Liberties of the Asiatic Women', *Asiatic Annual Register*, 1801.

Kinsley, D. *Hindu Goddesses: Visions of the Divine Feminine in the Hindu Religious Tradition*, Delhi, 1987.

Kishwar, M. and R. Vanita (eds.) *In Search of Answers: Indian Women's Voices from Manushi*, London, 1984.

Kishwar, M. 'Gandhi on Women', *Race and Class*, Summer 1986.
'The daughters of Aryavarta' in J. Krishnamurti (ed.) *Women in Colonial India: Survival, Work and the State*, Oxford University Press, Delhi, 1989.

Kolhatkar, W. 'Widow Remarriage' in C. Chintamani (ed.) *Indian Social Reform*, Madras, 1901.

Krishnamurti, J. (ed.) *Women in Colonial India: Survival, Work and the State*, Oxford University Press, Delhi 1989.

Lalita, K. et al (eds.) *We were Making History: Life Stories of Women in the Telengana People's Struggle*, London, 1989.

Lalita, K. et al (eds.) *An Anthology of Women's Writings, 1830–1897*, Kali for Women, New Delhi, 1992.

Leslie, J. *The Perfect Wife: The Orthodox Hindu Woman According to the Stridharmapaddhati of Tryambakayajvan*, Oxford Univeristy Press, Delhi, 1989.

Lokhande, N. *Panch Darpan: useful regulations of all the castes*, Bombay, 1876.

Lushington, J. 'On the Marriage rites and Usages of the Jats of Bharatpur', *Journal of the Asiatic Society*, 18, June 1833.

Malcolm, J. *A Memoir of Central India*, New Delhi, 1970.

Malshe, S.G. (ed.) *Kai. Tarabai Shindekrt Stri-purusha-tulana*, Mumbai Marathi Granthasangrahalaya, Bombay, 1975.

Mani, L. 'Contentious Traditions: The Debate on *Sati* in Colonial India' in K. Sangari and S. Vaid (eds.) *Recasting Women: Essays in Colonial History*, Kali for Women, New Delhi, 1989.

Marathe, K. *Naval va Natak yavishayi nibandha*, Bombay, 1872.

'A Memoir of the Bounsla family of Mahrattas', *Asiatic Annual Register*, 1801.

Molesworth, J.T. *A Dictionary, Marathi and English*, Bombay Education Society's Press, Bombay, 1857.

Moore, H. *Feminism and Anthropology*, Polity Press, Oxford, 1988.

Mullatti, L. *The Bhakti Movement and the Status of Women*, New Delhi, 1989.

Nanda, B. (ed.) *Indian Women from Purdah to Modernity*, New Delhi, 1975.

Nandy, A. *The Intimate Enemy: Loss and Recovery of Self under Colonialism*, Oxford University Press, Delhi 1983.

O'Hanlon, R. *Caste, Conflict and Ideology: Mahatma Jotirao Phule and Low Caste Protest in Nineteenth Century Western India*, Cambridge University Press, 1985.

——, 'Gender, Discourse and Resistance in Colonial Western India' in
    D. Haynes and G. Prakash (eds.) *Contesting Power: Resistance and
    Everyday Social Relations in South Asia*, Oxford University Press, Delhi
    1991.

Padval, T. *Jatibheda vivekasara*, Bombay 1865.

Papanek, H. and G. Minault (eds.) *Separate Worlds: Studies of Purdah in South
    Asia*, Delhi, 1982.

Papanek, H. 'Purdah: Separate Worlds and Symbolic Shelter' in H. Papanek
    and G. Minault (eds.) *Separate Worlds: Studies of Purdah in South Asia*,
    Delhi, 1982.

Patel, S. 'The Construction and Reconstruction of Woman in Gandhi', Nehru
    Memorial Museum and Library, *Occasional Papers in History and
    Society*, 49.

Perlin, F. 'Of White Whale and Countrymen in the Eighteenth Century
    Maratha Deccan: Extended Class Relations, Rights and the Problem of
    Rural Autonomy under the Old Regime', *Journal of Peasant Studies*, 5,
    2, 1978.

Phule, J. *Satsar*, in D. Keer and S.G. Malshe (eds.) *Mahatma Phule Samagra
    Vadmaya*, Bombay, 1969.

Pocock, D. 'Bases of faction in Gujarat', *British Journal of Sociology*,
    December, 1957.

Raeside, I. 'Agarkar, Apte and the Kanitkars', mimeo, n.d.
    'Early Prose Fiction in Marathi' in T. Clark (ed.) *The Novel in India: Its
    Birth and Development*, London, 1970.

Ramabai, Pandita, *Stridharmaniti*, Poona, 1882.
    The High Caste Hindu Woman, Bombay, 1982.

Ranade, M. *Rise of the Maratha Power*, New Delhi, 1970.

Ranade R. *Amchya ayushatil kahi athvani*, Bombay, 1910.

Ranade, R.D. *Mysticism in Maharashtra*, Delhi, 1982.

Raykar, S. (ed.) *Amhi Pahilele Phule*, Poona, 1981.

Risbud, N. *Manjughosha*, Poona, 1875.

Russell, R. and Rai Bahadur Hiralal (eds.) *The Tribes and Castes of Central
    India*, Calcutta, 1916.

Sangari, K. and S. Vaid (eds.) *Recasting Women: Essays in Colonial History*,
    Kali for Women, New Delhi, 1989.

Sardesai, G. *New History of the Marathas*, Bombay, 1868.

Sen, A. *Iswar Chandra Vidyasagar and his elusive milestones*, Calcutta, 1977.

Sengupta, P. *Pandita Ramabai Saraswati: Her Life and Work*, Asia Publishing
    House, Bombay, 1970.

Sherring, M. *Hindu Tribes and Castes as Represented in Benaras*, London
    1872.

Shinde, Tarabai. *Stri-purusha-tulana*, Poona, 1882.

Shridhar, *Pandavapratap*, Bombay, 1868.
    Ramavijaya, Bombay, 1876.

Sleeman, W. *Rambles and Recollections of an Indian Official*, London, 1893.

'Some Account of the Productions and Peculiarities of the Mahratta Country', Miscellaneous Tracts, *Asiatic Annual Register*, 1798–9.

Sontheimer, G. *The Hindu Joint Family*, New Delhi, 1977.

Steele, A. *The Law and Custom of Hindoo Castes within the Dekhun Provinces subject to the Presidency of Bombay*, London, 1868.

Tahmankar, D. *Lokamanya Tilak*, London, 1956.

Talwar, V. 'Feminist Consciousness in Women's Journals in Hindi' in K. Sangari and S. Vaid (eds.) *Recasting Women: Essays in Colonial History*, Kali for Women, New Delhi, 1989.

Tone, W. 'Illustrations of some Institutions of the Mahratta People', *Asiatic Annual Register*, 1799.

Tucker, R. 'From Dharmashastra to Politics', *Indian Social and Economic History Review*, 1970.

Vatuk, S. (ed.) *American Studies in the Anthropology of India*, New Delhi 1978.

Wadley, S. 'Women and the Hindu Tradition' in R. Ghadially (ed.) *Women in Indian Society*, New Delhi, 1988.

Washbrook, D. and B. Stein, 'States and societies: configuring state and capitalism in early modern India', mimeo, 1991.

Wink, A. *Land and Sovereignty in India: Agrarian Society and Politics under the Eighteenth Century Maratha Svarajya*, Cambridge University Press, 1986.

Wolpert, S.A. *Tilak and Gokhale: Revolution and Reform in the Making of Modern India*, University of California Press, Berkeley, 1961.

Index